Finding Our Compass

Finding Our Compass

Setting a course for Democracy to succeed

Robert Raymond

PALMETTO
P U B L I S H I N G
Charleston, SC
www.PalmettoPublishing.com

Paperback ISBN: 9798822959484
eBook ISBN: 9798822959491

TABLE OF CONTENTS

INTRODUCTION

"If you want to change the world, there's nothing to it."
—Gene Wilder

Change is a scary thing. The unknown consequences of change are the foundation of the fear of change. But there are unknown consequences to the status quo as well. And that is where we are now, facing the consequences of what we have known to be for a long time.

1—The two-party system in Politics is a prime example- how is that working for us now?

2—An Economy based on the principles of Free Market Capitalism- how is that working for us now?

3—The internet is a trusted source of factual information at our fingertips- that isn't true anymore.

All three of these examples are major components of our society that have been rolling right along and evolving without us really noticing or realizing it. They all started as a positive ideal and a positive force for the greater good. Now they have changed for the worse and the effects of their change has led to the consequences that almost brought down our Democracy and destroyed the United States of America as we know it.

Now is the time for fundamental changes to several of the components of our society. None of these changes will affect our Constitution or create a need to amend the Constitution in any way. The components of our society that I am going to propose changes to have led us to the end of a road. We are at a point in the evolution of America where we make the necessary changes, or our society will continue to rot where we are stuck now. The changes I am going to propose will set us down a new road with the knowledge that we need to pay attention and make little changes along the way so America can stay on a never-ending open road leading to a more prosperous and safer State of the Union.

We can make the changes I am going to propose with the understanding of the need for these changes, so they won't be scary. We can save our Democracy. We can return to being the shining light on the top of the hill. We can be the Country the World looks to as the gold standard of Democracy and not just another failed experiment doomed by human nature right from the beginning.

We are going to have to be firm in our resolve to make America a sustainable Democracy. There will be tremendous pushback from the elements that prosper on political divisiveness and culture wars. The business of division is a multi-billion-dollar industry. An industry that does not care about the success or failure of America. An industry that does not care about the well-being of Americans. There are radio and cable network opinion shows, there are podcasts and websites that make millions of dollars a year, getting Americans to distrust and hate one another. The proposals I will make will solve most of the issues that divide us. The industry of divisive rhetoric will be gutted and hopefully go away. Do not mistake what I am saying. I am not saying we need to end political and cultural debate. It is through the debate process that solutions and compromises can be found, established and woven into the healthy structure of a thriving Democracy.

The forces that want to dim the light of Democracy in America are global and domestic. There are foreign powers who see a successful Democracy in America as a threat to their autocratic hold on power in their country. Their biggest fear to their hold on power is a democratic uprising from their own people.

It is through foreign and domestic sources of misinformation that Americans are being led to believe that the other side of the political divide is evil. The consequence of allowing that to fester through the efforts of foreign and domestic operatives is the perception that America is a failing country and Democracy is to blame.

Together, we as Americans can dispel those perceptions and create a new narrative that America is thriving, and Democracy is to be celebrated. In this new age of the internet, we, as Americans, can show the world that we can turn off the lies. We, as Americans, can turn off the manipulation. We, as Americans, can strengthen Democracy around the World by strengthening our Democracy here in America. We can have news sources and media channels based on truth and facts.

"All our problems, they've got the same solution / Stop holding on, got to give into our evolution." That quote is from the song, "Revolution" by Dan Merrill.

It is time to create and choose a pathway forward. It is time to remove the wet blanket that has hindered our growth and development as a Society and a Nation. A blanket that is soaked with Racism, Intolerance, Greed, Self-interest, Misinformation, and Lies. We cannot choose to stay complacent in the face of these problems. We cannot choose to turn a blind eye to liars and their lies. We cannot choose to believe fiction over facts. We cannot choose to be played by others with their own best interest at stake.

It is time to call out those who are choosing to hold us down. I think we have the foundation to rise up and move forward. I believe we have Americans looking for a new path that cares about our fellow human beings and cares about healing and nurturing the planet we live on. The only planet we have to live on. The only planet our children and grandchildren will have to live on. There are physical forces much greater than our own that will shape our evolution for us, or we can choose to shape our evolution the best we can ourselves.

There are many ways to measure success, to raise the level of human existence in a world where nature is strong and healthy is probably the most successful thing we can do.

So, I ask you to please read this book with an open mind and consider a new path.

It is time to stop holding onto the path we have created and it is time to create a better path. Let's evolve into better human beings living in a better world created by us.

WHAT IS THE ROLE OF RELIGION IN A DEMOCRACY?

A lot of what divides us in this Country is the differences in our religious beliefs. Issues such as Abortion, Gay Marriage, and Transgender Rights are examples of religious issues that create huge divides between Americans. And since we are all entitled to have our own religious beliefs, there is no right or wrong in anyone's position on these issues.

In the Constitution, the First Amendment does two things as it relates to the freedom of Religion:

"Congress shall make no law respecting an establishment of religion, or prohibiting the free exercise thereof…"

The First Amendment keeps the Government from forcing us to live under the umbrella of a specific Religion, and the First Amendment allows us to choose and stay true to a Religion of our choice.

I think before we go on, we should define the difference between Religion and God. I know that may sound unnecessary, but I believe it needs to be spelled out. If we can understand the difference between the two then we will be able to accept one into our public life and save the other one for our private life.

A Religion is the collection of the beliefs of what God is, what God stands for, and what God expects from us as human beings. Religions are formed and founded as people with similar beliefs come together as a group.

God is one of the names that refer to a Supreme Being. God is the name used in Christianity. There are other names for the Supreme Being used in other Religions. And there are many other names within Christianity itself that refer to God. But please forgive me as I am going to use the word "God" to represent the Supreme Being I believe in. And I mean no disrespect to anyone else who may have a different name for the Supreme Being they choose to believe in. I can only speak to what I believe in as it pertains to "God."

Most Religions refer to their Supreme Being to be the one that has created all that they know to exist and is the architect of all that they will know in the future. There is no absolute, undeniable evidence that proves the existence of a Supreme Being. The belief in the existence of a Supreme Being is based in faith and faith alone. The shared faith of individuals gives them a sense of belonging, a sense of worth, and a sense of security. And with all that comes an innate desire to protect the group and all they share. It is due to the innate desire to protect the group that we struggle to accept beliefs different from our own. We struggle in our acceptance of other religions because we feel if we validate their beliefs, somehow that invalidates our own. But that is not the case at all; actually accepting someone else's beliefs and them accepting yours only validates your shared commitment to honoring the loving God you each believe in.

We have the idea of God mentioned in the founding documents of our Nation. "In God We Trust" is on our currency. There can be no separation between Government and the core ideals expected from us by God. Yet there must be a separation between Government and the conflicting ideals of different Religions.

I believe there is a place and a role for God in our Government. But there is no place and no role for Religion in the way we govern. Government cannot get into the business of sanctioning certain religions. The First Amendment strives to keep a person's religious beliefs private and non-intrusive to another person's religious beliefs.

Whether you believe in the existence of God or you don't believe in the existence of God, you have a sense of what is right and what is wrong. What is just and what is unjust. In most Religions it is through the God the people believe in that delineates what they believe to be fair and what they believe to be unfair, what they believe to be just, and what they believe to be unjust. Aren't the answers to what is fair and what is just the essence of what God stands for, what each of our Gods stands for? Believers in God and non-believers in God share a lot of the same values and want a government built on the ideals of decency and fairness. Whether you believe in God or you don't believe in God, you probably believe we should have laws that protect humanity and each other. The best ideals of what God expects from us and the best ideals of humanity without religion are very close to being one and the same.

"My religion cannot tolerate Abortion, and so I can't tolerate another religion that does." I understand that sentiment. I get where they are coming from. But they don't have to tolerate the other person's religious beliefs by making them their own. But the Government has to tolerate different religious beliefs and make sure that people have the right to believe in them.

I have tried to teach my children that trying to prove you're right isn't always the right thing to do. After all, it is possible that both sides of an issue may be right.

I understand that the meaning of what is Right, Just, and Fair can be debated. But I also know the closer we come to a compromise, the closer we come to what is Right and Just and Fair for everyone.

We don't want people to be forced to do what their religious beliefs don't want them to do. We don't want them baking cakes or taking pictures at an event they don't believe in or want to be at. People should not be forced to give up their religious beliefs to accommodate someone else's. We need to find a compromise that will keep this issue from being used to divide us. Issues such as this one are often used as a component to further a larger agenda to divide us even more and to sow the seeds of hate. Aren't we the fools if we let others manipulate us into hating each other for their own gain?

Let's talk about a compromise when it comes to protecting people's religious freedoms when they conflict with someone else's religious beliefs. We know we don't want someone to be forced to participate in an event their religious beliefs won't allow. And on the other hand, people should not be forced to feel humiliated when being discriminated against when they are being denied products or services because of their religious beliefs. We need to find a way for everyone to be true to the God they believe in and not have people be forced to feel discriminated against and humiliated in public.

But how do we do that? I used to think if you applied for a business license you would have to agree not to discriminate against those people whose rights are protected by law. How do we let a business owner say, "I can't sell you products or services because you are gay. I can't plan your wedding because it is an interracial arrangement. I can't make you a cake because you are Catholic. I can't photograph your wedding because you are Jewish or Muslim"? But the Supreme Court, in the case of *Masterpiece Cakeshop vs. Colorado Civil Rights Commission*, weighed in and pretty much said business owners could use their religious beliefs as an excuse not to offer products or services to religious events they do not agree with. And I agree with them on the issue.

I believe there is a way to protect both parties: one party from being forced to take part in a religious event they don't believe in and protect the other party from feeling discriminated against by being refused products or services based on their religious beliefs.

The solution is that, when applying for a business license, the applicant will need to decline or declare a need for an exemption from anti-discrimination laws based on their religious beliefs. These exemptions would only be granted to the business owner and the business as they pertain to a conflict with a consumer's religious belief. The bottom line is a Place of Business would be granted an exemption from having to provide a product or service to be used at a religious event that is in conflict with the Business Owner's religious beliefs. Publicly held companies would not be able to ascertain such an exemption, nor would a business be entitled to retain such an exemption once it has become a publicly traded company based on the diverse religious beliefs held by its shareholders.

Once a business owner is granted an exemption, the business owner will need to display a sticker or placard at each point of entry to their place of business, including online websites. The sticker or placard will alert the potential customer to what types of religious events the place of business chooses not to participate in. That will protect the potential customers from feeling discriminated against and humiliated in public. Failing to display proper signage with regard to the religious exemption would result in fines and/or the loss of their business license for multiple offenses. This would allow both parties to be able to stay true to their religious beliefs and the consumer would be free to seek out products or services without fear of public discrimination.

I believe it is important that business owners have the right not to have their business participate in religious events they are opposed to participating in. However, under no circumstances would an employee have the right to their own exemption. An employee would be considered a representative of the business they are employed at and would have to abide by the exempt or non-exempt status of the business itself and follow the guidelines set forth by the business license granted to the owner.

I am not a lawyer and certainly wouldn't want to pretend to be one. But I would like to propose a law that would put a policy in place. Let's keep in mind that this is only a draft, subject to editing by true Constitutional lawyers, so it will stand the test of time. I believe such a law can be passed at the Federal level.

Re: Freedom From Religion Act

"The Government shall not compel a privately owned business that provides products or services to participate in a religious event that conflicts with the religious exemptions the business has established. Businesses that choose exempt status from discrimination laws based on their religious beliefs shall be forced to display their exempt status at the points of entry into their business whether those points of entry are at a physical location or the points of entry are at a virtual storefront."

There is going to be pushback from both sides of the issue.

The obvious pushback will be, "Why would we allow people to discriminate against other law-abiding, God-fearing human beings who have done nothing wrong except try and secure products or services for their religious event?" The answer is in the fact that each and every Religion strives to stand tall and above other Religions. And for that reason, we cannot ask someone to go against their own religious beliefs because, after all, their religious beliefs stand tall and above other religions to them.

Another form of pushback will come in the opinion that the Law doesn't go far enough and protect an individual's right from having to participate in another person's religious event. Why wouldn't the same reasoning that applies to places of business apply to individuals? An employee is rendered to be a representative of the business and must abide by its policies as stated at the time of licensing or relicensing. When a person accepts a job, they are expected to carry out the responsibilities that come with the job. A person cannot claim a personal exemption from meeting the job requirements based on religious beliefs. Those religious beliefs would make them unqualified for the job right from the start. It is for that reason that exemptions cannot be given to individuals. I think we can all agree that individuals do not have a right to a job where they can't perform the responsibilities that come with the job.

Can we address another religious issue that is used to divide us into hating each other? Saying the word "Christmas" in public. How did saying "Merry Christmas" become such a terrible thing? How does having a Christmas tree in public cause such an uproar that it is said to be unconstitutional? The whole issue is framed to be an attack on Christianity. I don't blame people for getting defensive and sticking up for their right to be a Christian. And I don't blame people for trying to protect the First Amendment and not wanting to see Christianity established as a State Religion. This issue is easily used to create division among people who are both trying to do the right thing.

To a Christian, Christianity is a religion that stands tall and above all other religions and is worth standing up and fighting for. To a Patriotic American, the Constitution is worth standing up and fighting for. How do we find a compromise? Rooted deep in the foundation of any difficult compromise are the components of acceptance and tolerance. And this compromise will be no exception.

If someone wants to wish you a Merry Christmas, and you are not a Christian, accept it as a greeting of goodwill. Tolerate the fact they didn't have any concern that you may not be a Christian but are wishing you God's love for the Holiday Season.

It's ok to say Merry Christmas, Happy Hanukkah, or Happy Kwanzaa. Whatever holiday you are celebrating, it's ok to share the goodwill that comes with celebrating that Holiday. People need to recognize you are sharing your love for your Holiday with them and not trying to put your Religion upon them. If someone shares their religious greeting with you…smile…and share your religious greeting with them. Sharing a smile and a sincere greeting of God's love can only bring us closer as human beings.

It is so important to realize that those people who fault you for saying the all-encompassing greeting of Happy Holidays instead of saying Merry Christmas are willing pawns or unwitting participants in a broader scheme to divide us and further a larger agenda. I cannot stress enough the importance of taking the time to recognize those people who are trying to divide us and sow the seeds of hate and choosing not to be persuaded into hating your fellow Americans. We can choose to love one another instead of being manipulated into hating each other for someone else's gain. The business of division and hate is a multi-billion-dollar business that certain people are not going to give up easily. But, we together, acting as one, can put them out of business.

I don't think it matters what your religious beliefs are when it comes to having a tree that is beautifully decorated. I think everyone loves the sight of a Holiday Tree. You can call your tree whatever you want: call it a Christmas Tree or call it a Holiday Tree. But be assured that any tree put up in the town square or on city property must be an all-encompassing Holiday Tree. A symbol of the season for everyone to enjoy. A reminder to all of us of the importance of sharing love, kindness, and compassion with those of you who are different from ourselves. Yet any tree put up by a place of business or a company held as public or private can be called whatever the place of business or company wants to call it. The Rockefeller Center Christmas Tree is a prime example of that and is always a beautiful sight and an inspiration for us to treat others with the love, kindness, and compassion that Christ would want us to. And, just as easily, a Christmas tree can be viewed as a symbol of the Holiday Season and nothing more. We have the freedom to view anything in any way we choose. But we do not have the right to force that view onto someone else.

God, known by any name, must be welcomed and celebrated in our society. Religions must be shared and held private by individuals. There is no role for Religion in a Democracy other than to give its citizens a source of serenity and faith. The individuals that do not believe in God can choose to see the word God as a symbol for all that is Just and Fair in the ways we treat one another. There are choices we can make in the ways we accept another person's religious faith or we accept another person's lack of faith. Making choices that improve our lives and the lives of others that we disagree with seems like an easy choice to make.

Let's take the love that God expects us to share or our longing for what is Just and Right without faith and share it with each other. Let's incorporate it into the structure of our government and into the laws that protect our lives and liberty.

We can set a course to create a Country where God and what is Right and Just are woven into our society to make our lives better.

GUNS

Every day in America, there is an average of 218 people shot with a firearm, and an average of 118 of those who are shot will die. Every day in America, an average of 17 children and/or teens are shot with a gun, and an average of 5 of those who are shot will die from their wounds. I sourced these statistics from a website called Gun Violence Archive at gunviolencearchive.org.

I want all of you to stop and imagine what it would be like to lose a friend or family member to gun violence. And realize that it probably took time for them to die. And imagine what your loved one was feeling and thinking as they began to take their last few breaths, knowing they were about to die. Imagine that person being your son or daughter. As sad as that would be and as angry as you would feel before your deep sense of grief sets in, you need to remember that guns don't kill people; people kill people. Guns are not the problem; people are the problem.

So, what should we do about guns? What do we do about gun violence?

What should our goals be as they pertain to gun control? Let's try and figure that out.

First Goal…and the most important of our goals is to ensure the Right for law-abiding citizens to own a gun.

Second Goal…is to reduce gun violence by keeping guns out of the hands of people who shouldn't own a gun.

Third Goal…is to punish those people who commit crimes using a gun and to punish those people whose guns were used to commit a crime.

That's it. I believe it's that simple.

Let's talk about the Second Amendment and how it has been interpreted. The Court's position has been steadfast that American Citizens have the right to own a gun. The Court has been steadfast that there are reasons that would prevent a person from owning a gun. If someone has a mental illness that may prevent them from being able to own a gun. If someone has a violent past or is awaiting trial for a violent crime that may prevent them from being able to own a gun. If we can pull out the phrase in the Second Amendment, "The right of the people to keep and bear Arms, shall not be infringed," and make that the law of the land. Then we can pull out the words "well regulated" and make that the policy of the land. In order to please most everyone on both sides of the issue, we need to ensure a person's right to bear arms and we need to regulate the manner in which they do so.

How do we accomplish that? How do we please most everyone on both sides of the issue?

Treat guns the same way we treat automobiles. We have laws in place for automobiles because we have determined they are deadly weapons that can cause property damage and death if used irresponsibly. But we don't treat guns the same way even though they are manufactured with the sole purpose of being a deadly weapon.

If we take all of our laws that pertain to automobiles as a deadly weapon and treat guns the same way, we will be able to accomplish all our goals. Take all of our laws that pertain to automobiles with respect to personal liability and treat guns the same way. Take all of our laws that pertain to owning and registering an automobile and treat guns the same way. Take all of our laws that pertain to transferring ownership of an automobile and treat guns the same way. Take all the laws as they pertain to the liability of damages caused by your automobile being loaned to someone else, and do the same for guns.

Some people might say, "We can't do that. It would take a whole new bureaucracy and be too expensive."

No, it doesn't, and no, it wouldn't. Too simple of a response? Let me explain and you may agree.

We take the locations of the Department of Motor Vehicles at the State level and turn them into the Department of Motor Vehicles and Firearms (DMVF) at a Federal level. Automobiles and Firearms can cross State lines with no regard to the laws and regulations of the individual States. It seems to make sense to put them under a Federal umbrella.

The only thing we need to do is add a little box onto the automobile registration form that says "firearm." And check the box when a firearm is being registered. The make, model, and serial number boxes are already there. The form is already complete, otherwise.

What is even more beautiful about this idea is the information with regards to gun registration will be readily available to law enforcement. The same database that manages driver licenses and car registrations will also manage firearm registration.

There will be a big pushback from some gun owners who will say that gun registration is the first step to gun confiscation. We can't let those people distract us from our goals. Using the fear of gun confiscation to further an agenda of division and hate is shameful. The Second Amendment protects the Right to own a gun, period. The Government at the State level or the Federal level cannot and would not ever come for the guns of a law-abiding citizen. I know there are people out there who want to see guns go away. They want handguns to be illegal. They do not understand why we have to have handguns. Handguns are used for protection.

A popular tactic used to divide us and get us to hate each other is to portray the voices of a few as the voices of the many. Let's be realistic; most Americans believe we need to do more to reduce the amount of gun violence.

As long as we ensure everyone's right to own a gun legally, we can find a compromise. Background checks are easy through the DMVF database. We will have to require additional agencies to report to the DMVF any irregularities as to why someone shouldn't be allowed to own a gun. We already require medical institutions to report why a person can't drive a car temporarily for medical reasons. We can add other agencies to report reasons as well. For example, a history of violent crimes, mental illness, ties to terrorism, or that they are under a certain type of restraining order as ordered by a Judge.

How does this policy of treating guns like automobiles reduce gun violence? It makes it harder for a person to obtain a gun who isn't legally allowed to obtain a gun.

"Sure, but people will find a way to get a gun anyway." That's true at first…but it will be a crime for a person to sell someone a gun without the proper laws being followed, and the person it is registered to will be on the hook for a certain level of liability for any crime that gun is used in. "They will file off the serial number, and it won't be traceable." I bet we can find a way to make them all traceable.

I would have to believe that law enforcement would be in favor of this added information at their fingertips. Wouldn't it be nice for a police officer to know the car they are about to pull over is registered to a person who owns several weapons? How about when police officers are called to a residence, they can be enroute and find out how many and what type of weapons are registered to the people living at that address? In the day-to-day lives of police officers on the streets, this type of information would be valuable and save lives.

So how do we structure these new regulations with regard to gun shows and personal sales?

The Department of Motor Vehicles and Firearms would have a booth at all gun shows, and the sales and background checks would be finalized at their booth. All gun shows would have to be permitted beforehand to ensure the availability of a DMVF booth on the premises.

Store sales would have access to a DMVF website that would allow for instant background checks, and, if the purchaser passes the background check, they would be instantly registered as the owner of the firearm and assume all the responsibilities that entails.

Private Sales would have to be conducted at the DMVF with both parties present to absolve the seller of any liability in case the gun is used in a crime. There would be no record of the purchase amount, only a record of the transfer of ownership. This makes it very hard for a criminal to obtain a gun through a private sale. It would be unlikely that a potential criminal or a wanted criminal would go into a DMVF and try to obtain ownership of a gun. It is this particular aspect of the law that closes the manner in which most criminals receive their weapons: through private sales.

Putting guns under the umbrella of Tort Laws, as automobiles are, is the first step to preventing a gun owner from ignoring the process at the DMVF. Using the Negligent Entrustment cause of action as it pertains to automobiles and putting that onto the sales or lending of guns is the second step. What that means is that a person who owns a gun and lends it to someone else who then uses the gun in a crime, or that gun is used in an accidental shooting, the owner of the gun is open to civil liability or possibly criminal negligence. It also means a person who sells a gun to someone else and the ownership of the gun is not legally transferred to the buyer, and if the gun is used in a crime or accidental shooting, the last known owner of the gun is open to civil liability or criminal negligence. This will be a big help to keeping guns out of the hands of people who are not legally eligible to own a gun. Because who would want to illegally sell a gun or lend a gun to someone and be on the hook for what happens with that gun?

I really believe this is a compromise we can agree on. The laws would actually strengthen a person's right to legally own a gun and, at the same time, help keep guns out of the hands of people who have been deemed to be too unsafe to own a gun.

The only way we can achieve this goal is to keep our heads down and vote for people who agree this is the direction to go in.

A well-regulated "right of the people to keep and bear arms" is a great compromise for us to reach and lower the amount of gun violence in America.

We can set a course where guns are used for sport and protection but never tolerated in crime or violence.

MISINFORMATION: A SLOW-ACTING POISON POISED TO UNDERMINE AMERICA'S FORM OF DEMOCRACY

We can't understand the effects of misinformation without knowing what it is. What is misinformation? The Webster Dictionary online defines it as "incorrect or misleading information." That's a pretty simple definition, powerful in its meaning but soft on the surface.

Incorrect information…is information that is wrong or false.

Misleading information…is incorrect information that may lead to a false conclusion.

When misinformation is purposely portrayed as factual and true, it is very difficult for us to see it for what it is: a lie that is intended to manipulate us to achieve an end. The people who are putting forth the misinformation are betting we won't take the time to fact-check their misinformation. And, when the misinformation is put forth time and time again and left unchallenged, your subconscious begins to file it as true.

A perfect example of the power of misinformation is that there are lots of people who now believe newscasts are full of fake news. They believe that the major news networks are lying to the American people. I can assure you that the business model behind the network evening news does not include fake news or lying. That would destroy a business model that makes a boatload of money for the network. Yes, there have been instances when the major news networks were duped into portraying a story that was completely inaccurate.

A great example of that was the confrontation between Nick Sandmann and Nathan Phillips on the steps of the Lincoln Memorial. You may remember the story and the picture of the MAGA hat-wearing teenager face-to-face with a drum-beating Native American. The teenager was portrayed as confronting the Native American when, actually, the facts were just the opposite. That moment was used by people to portray the major news outlets as peddling misinformation and peddling fake news. The mainstream media fell for the partial video and ran with a story that wasn't true. The incident and others like it have had a profound effect on the credibility of network news. But that doesn't mean they purposely misrepresent the facts of a story or peddle fake news. There have been news anchors disciplined for lying or knowingly perpetuating falsehoods: Brian Williams, Dan Rather and Lara Logan, for example. And certain Fox News Hosts have admitted to knowingly lying to their audience about the 2020 election results. But when you think of all the news stories that are put out there and all the people who are waiting to jump on a story and expose it as false or fake, it is very rare that any stories are actually proven to be false. Can I repeat that, please? It is extremely rare that any stories are actually proven to be false.

When you take the news industry in its entirety and the huge amount of factual information they put out, and to have so few instances of providing misinformation with or without the intent to mislead, it is very difficult to accuse them of peddling fake news. The ironic fact about fake news is that the whole story of fake news is being perpetrated by people disseminating misinformation to achieve their desired goal. Because if you don't believe the news media, then the news media can't expose people in power for corruption or breaking the law. Imagine someone having the goal to be able to break the law and embezzle billions of dollars from the American taxpayer, and the news media breaks the story and isn't believed by millions of Americans. The Department of Justice starts an investigation into corrupt Government officials, and that investigation is labeled as a Deep State fake investigation. The story of a fake investigation is put forth with misinformation, and millions of Americans are led to believe it to be true. That starts to build a foundation where people in power can operate with impunity. If your values are like mine, and you believe we should protect the Rule of Law and preserve our Democracy and the Constitution of the United States, then we need to seek out a way to provide a protected source of fact-based news. Hannah Arendt said it best; "The moment we no longer have a free press, anything can happen. What makes it possible for a totalitarian or any other dictatorship to rule is that people are not informed."

Another example of the powerful effect of misinformation is that millions and millions of voters in the 2020 Presidential election believe the election was rigged and stolen. Which isn't true. There are always voter irregularities in every election. An election worker checks off the name of a dead person still on the voting rolls instead of checking off the person with the same name standing right in front of them. But the crux of the misinformation put out there was that people voted more than once. There were so many ballots mailed out that people would decide to break the law and vote more than once. And there was no evidence of that. The Courts were forced to dismiss lawsuit after lawsuit for lack of evidence or lack of any legal standing. Yet, with all the misinformation put out there, millions of people believe it was a stolen election, and nothing could be further from the truth. The election was not stolen. There is zero evidence that it was. Think of the resources spent to prove otherwise, spent to prove it was stolen. And, to this day, they still haven't provided any substantial evidence that it was stolen. But the misinformation has convinced millions of Americans otherwise.

I called into my local radio talk show to comment on the subject of how one candidate could get 80 million votes. I talked about my neighbor, who is a lifelong Republican and voted Democrat at the top of the ticket. I talked about the effect the pandemic had on expanding early voting and voting by mail. I talked about voting districts that typically have too few voting places with too few machines, and I talked about the people in those voting districts who don't typically vote because it takes too long. Those people were able to vote early or by mail and have their voices heard. Then, out of nowhere, one of the radio hosts asked me about the 60,000 votes in Georgia that were cast by 15-year-olds. He said he saw it online, and it was said in a Senate hearing, so it had to be true. I had to laugh, and I calmly said that just because someone says something doesn't make it true. I have seen Congressmen on the Floor of the House or Senate outright lie about the facts of something. The purpose is not to try and convince their colleagues into believing the lie; it is so it can be played time and time again online and used as propaganda to manipulate Americans into believing the lie. We need to vote those liars out of office. Do we really want liars representing us in Congress? They have the right to lie. The First Amendment doesn't just protect truthful speech; it protects most speech, including lies. Congressmen and women have the right to tell lies on the floor of the Senate or House chambers with no recourse because our Constitution protects their right to do so. But we can call them out on it. We can report and document their lies, and we can document their misinformation designed to fool you, trick you, and mislead you. And we can vote them out.

And we have a new phenomenon where people want to be lied to and want to be told what they want to believe, no matter how false it is. That was no more apparent than when a cable news company fired a top-rated host for a number of legitimate reasons that any other company would have fired an employee for. The backlash of his firing was directed at the news company. The host, who has made a career out of lying to his target audience, was defended by his audience. They chose to take out their anger over his firing on the cable news corporation. They chose to not watch the news channel and cancel their subscriptions to their online news service. Instead of being mad at the host for lying to them and playing them for fools, they chose to be mad at the news channel for firing him, they chose to be mad at the news channel for doing the right thing. What that showed me was that there is a large number of people out there who would rather be lied to and played for fools so long as they hear what they want to believe instead of being told the truth. I am not sure how to combat that. I have to think the only way to combat that is to show those people who want to believe the misinformation the benefit of knowing the truth and how the truth benefits them.

One of our first callings is to make sure we vote no matter how hard it becomes to vote. Make sure we vote out anyone who makes it harder to vote. Protecting our right to vote needs to be this Nation's top priority, because if we can't vote out the liars, then we can't stop the lies or the misinformation put forth to destroy our Democracy. Do we want to be the generation that lets the greatest experiment in the history of civilization fail?

A cable news corporation built a business model that would use misinformation put forth in an online periodical or a blog and create a news segment based on that misinformation. Next thing you know, because they were peddling so much misinformation, it had an effect on the political discourse in America. And I believe that is what has led to this new phenomenon of people wanting to be lied to instead of being told the truth.

Fast forward to today, and now there is so much misinformation about politics that is coming from so many news sources that a person doesn't know what to believe. And that has led to people believing what they want to believe instead of believing what is factual and true. When you have two different sets of facts that are believed to be true, it is hard for people to find common ground or reach a compromise.

I absolutely love the saying, "You are entitled to your own opinion, but you are not entitled to your own facts." The truth is the truth, and the facts are the facts. Period. There are no exceptions.

That is a perfect segway to solving this problem. How do we differentiate between opinion and fact? We must keep in mind that facts are facts and nothing more. However, opinions can come in many forms.

Opinion can be an intellectual assessment of the facts. Opinion can be an assessment of an alternate set of facts put forth as misinformation.

Opinion can be used as a vehicle to purposely spread misinformation to achieve a goal. Opinion can come from an honest place in the heart. Opinion can come from a nefarious place in the mind. It doesn't matter where it comes from, it is only an opinion. It is a point of view put forth to support the truth or to undermine the truth.

If we can have a rating system for movies and television programs, then we can have a rating system for news programs and talk shows. We have rating systems for movies and television shows that inform you of content. We need to do that for news programs and talk shows.

The rating systems for movies and television shows inform you of content such as sexual situations, violence, and strong language. The rating system for news programs and talk shows needs to inform you whether the content is based in fact, opinion, or opinion based in fact.

In America people have the Constitutionally protected right to free speech. They have the right to lie to you, they have the right to misinform you, and they have the right to verbally manipulate you into believing something that is not true to benefit themselves or others. That is the ugly side of free speech. But they do not have the right to incite you into violence. They do not have the right to order you to commit violence. The Right to Free Speech is not absolute. People will try to convince you otherwise. They will say they have the right to free speech and they cannot be censored. There is a struggle going on with Facebook deciding to label that certain posts may not be factual or true. The reason that people are trying to fight such labeling is because they are spreading misinformation. These types of platforms are trying to bend the curve toward truth and facts. They have recognized that their platforms are being used to spread lies and misinformation. Their platforms are being used to fester a false reality that can lead to social unrest and violence, and they have the right to say, "Not on my platform." They recognize their platforms are being used to pit Americans against Americans through the spreading of misinformation. They have the right as a corporation to choose not to be used to spread lies and misinformation. Then we see they have the right to sell their platform to someone who chooses to allow misinformation on their platform to further an end to our Democracy as we know it. We, as Americans, can choose not to use their platform. We can choose to be Pro-American, Pro-Truth, and Pro-Democracy.

No one could have ever imagined that we could have so many elected leaders in this country that are peddling lies and misinformation. It is this type of political misinformation that is poisoning our form of Democracy in America. I cannot believe these elected people keep getting re-elected. It shows a dangerous level of belief in a false narrative based on lies and misinformation. I would never vote for a person who repeatedly lies to me and the American people. But when false information is presented in a factual manner, how can you tell what is factual and what is misinformation?

We won't be able to rate and label all programs that present themselves as news programs. We won't be able to rate and label all shows that present themselves as talk shows. There are way too many platforms and shows out there—there are over 800,000 active podcasts alone. So how do we rate, label, and monitor so many shows having so much content on any given day? We don't, because we can't.

Instead of the FCC trying to rate, label, and monitor all the content out there, the news programs and talk shows will sign up and register to be rated, labeled, and monitored as fact based. No one is going to volunteer to be rated untruthful or misleading. And we do not want to get into the business of labeling a broadcast as untruthful or misleading. But we can rate, label, and monitor news broadcasts that desire to be labeled as news programs based in fact, and we can do the same for talk shows that desire to be labeled talk shows based in truth and fact.

I believe there is a tremendous market out there for the truth and the facts. I believe people want the facts about both sides of a story in a common reality. I believe the business model of programming based on truth and facts would be very successful. There are business models out there already putting forth shows and broadcasts based on truth and facts. But when you have people and organizations constantly labeling those programs as Fake News, then you will have people beginning to believe those programs are full of lies and misinformation. When the reality is just the opposite. Imagine being a wonderful, honest human being who cares about helping those people around them to be better people. Imagine being a wonderful, caring human being who only wants to make America the best country it can be, and you are labeled and branded a liar, an evil person, and a threat to society. The misinformation campaign against you is so persistent and effective that people around you begin to believe it is true. It would be enough to make you feel hopeless and defeated.

For the news programs and talk shows that want to be rated as being based in fact and truth, these programs and shows would register with the FCC and pay to be monitored. They would then have a symbol superimposed on their broadcast to show they are rated as fact based and are being monitored by the FCC. The FCC would monitor all broadcasts registered to be labeled as fact based. I believe it is essential for the American people to have a source of news and opinion shows based in a common reality that is based in truth and facts.

Of course there would be penalties for presenting misinformation. If there are too many violations and a disregard for presenting a program based in fact, then their rating would be taken away. However, there would be a vehicle for arbitration and a road to the reinstatement of a truthful rating.

Unfortunately, we live in a world of conflicting realities, one based in fact and one based on misinformation. If we continue to let misinformation be presented as truthful and factual, then there is a good chance we will see violent unrest, as both sides see themselves as Just and Righteous. The really difficult part of seeing through all the misinformation is that there are multiple actors, both foreign and domestic, that present the misinformation as truthful and factual. And the business of misinformation is a multi-billion-dollar business that will not go away without a fight. Whenever people are making tens of millions of dollars, they do not care how much harm they bring to fellow Americans. They do not care how much hatred and division they cause. The business revenue of hatred and division is in the billions of dollars. People will not give that up without a fight. It disgusts me that people make so much money getting Americans to hate fellow Americans by lying to them.

How do we purge the misinformation that causes hatred and division from our society? It seems to be impossible, but I don't believe it is. We give Americans a place to go and be confident that their News shows, Talk shows, and Opinion shows are based in truth and fact. Capitalism is a tremendous force. Money is power. Capitalism is a simple system: nothing happens until something is sold or a service is paid for. If the business models of division and hate are no longer profitable, then the business models of division and hate will go away. But consumers and corporations need to be vigilant in their battle not to accept or enable the business model of hate to be profitable. The truth is, once the profits are gone, all you will have left is a bunch of liars with no platform to lie.

They say all politicians lie; that might be true, but I don't believe it is. Just because you say one thing during the campaign and then vote for something different, that doesn't make you a liar. Isn't the essence of a compromise when two parties move off their position and meet somewhere in the middle, meet somewhere other than where they started from? I do not believe all politicians tell big lies or that all politicians tell small lies. But the one thing I do know is that there are politicians that do tell big lies and do tell small lies. People don't usually have to lie to further an agenda that is Right and Just. What should we do with politicians that lie to us? Vote them out. What do we do with advertisers who advertise on platforms designed to mislead and lie to us? We can choose not to do business with those companies who endorse platforms used to mislead and lie to us, pitting Americans against Americans for their own gain and America's demise.

We can set a course to a place where we can find the truth and facts so we can make decisions that improve our lives.

THE ECONOMY

"We need an economy that works for all Americans, not just those at the top." Have you heard that before? What does that mean? No one has ever explained it. It sounds great. An economy where everyone has a fair chance to be successful. Isn't that what people expect, and isn't that what people want? Shouldn't the American Dream be achievable by working hard and being rewarded for that hard work, whether it be working for yourself or working for someone else?

If we are going to build an economy that works for everyone, we need to govern by the rule and not the exception. A Government cannot run an economy by trying to make it perfectly fair for everyone. Economies are too big and too complicated. The best way a government can run an economy is to set policy that keeps as many people participating in the economy as possible and to have those people participate at the highest possible level they can. That means making sure the people who are going to spend their money, typically your lower and middle classes, are able to acquire enough currency to pay their bills and have extra to spend on clothes, dining, and recreation.

A friend of mine recently went to a foreign country for a month just to vacation and hang out in his ancestor's homeland. I asked him what he thought was the biggest difference in the quality of life between that Country and America. And what he told me was not what I had expected to hear. He said people living in this other country work so they can have extra money to enjoy life, travel, and have leisure time with their children and families. Here in America, people work hard to just stay alive and to just to get by. It didn't make sense to me at first, but then I realized what he meant. He meant that in the other country, people would work and make enough money so they could afford to travel and have adventures—to feel alive. But in America, most people work hard and are only able to pay their bills. They work hard to pay the bills for their basic needs. There isn't enough extra money to travel, to experience adventure. In America, most of us work hard just to pay the bills and get by. That is all that most of us are capable of in our economy, and, for some reason, we are made to feel ashamed for that. We are working hard and barely getting by so others can accumulate great wealth. That doesn't seem fair.

I think we need to develop an Economic system where every hard-working American can afford to enjoy their life. Probably one of the greatest gifts that we can give back to God is to ensure most people have the time and means to enjoy their lives.

So how do we create an economic system that accomplishes that?

Let's start with a mission statement: "Give people the ability to work hard and enjoy life."

We need an economic system that has a foundation structured in Capitalism. We need an economic system that fuels its own economic engine. We cannot keep printing money and injecting it into the economy. We cannot keep extending credit to people who can't afford to pay it back. Those are not the ways to fuel a sustainable economy and to achieve steady growth.

The term Capitalism was coined not that long ago, in the mid-19th century. The term was coined at the time that Socialism was coined as well. It was a time when people were trying to label different types of economies and define the principles those economies were based on.

Webster's online dictionary defines Capitalism as follows: "An economic system characterized by private or corporate ownership of capital goods; by investments that are determined by private decisions; and by prices, production and distribution of goods that are determined mainly by competition in a free market."

That seems to me to be the definition of a type of Capitalism called Free Market Capitalism. Free Market Capitalism is a system that seems to be what we have aspired to make work for America. And I believe most of us would agree that in America, in the modern age of Big Business, it has reached a point where Free Market Capitalism is failing us and needs to be adjusted and fixed. It is the size of Big Business that has eliminated the benefit of competition, which is a cornerstone to the success of Free Market Capitalism.

I think the definition of Capitalism should be: "An economic system in which an individual or a group of individuals are able to sell products or services in exchange for currency." The definition needs to be simple and concise.

Wage earners would fall into the category of selling a service; their service would be their labor in exchange for currency.

My goal in this chapter is to define and structure an economic system that feeds its own success through the definition of Capitalism that I laid out. And it is through this system that we can have an economy that works for everyone. The American Dream is to work hard, and you can have a good life. And everyone has the right to define what is their own "good life." For some it will be a rich, lavish life; for others it will be a more simple and less stressful life.

We are going to call my economic system "Oak Tree Economics." It will be structured in a foundation of capitalism without the failed Free Market principles to slow it down.

The engine of Oak Tree Economics is fueled by the demand for products and services. Nothing happens in an economy based on the structure of Capitalism until something is bought or sold.

Oak Tree Economics will be an economic system that feeds itself so it can continue to grow and thrive, much like an Oak Tree that drops its leaves, and the leaves in turn fertilize the soil. Trees cannot search for food, so they produce their own food for growth. How about we create an economy that feeds itself? One that rewards hard work with enough wealth to enjoy life. Not an economy where you work hard just to stay alive.

I want you to picture an Oak tree solidly rooted in its soil. And picture the tree with many main branches and many other branches coming off of those main branches. Now I want to break down the different components of the tree and how they relate to the economy I want us to build:

—The soil around the tree is symbolic of the consumers in the economy.

—The roots of the tree are symbolic of the point of sale for goods and services.

—The trunk of the tree is symbolic of the vehicle in which commerce is conducted and wealth is exchanged. Wealth being redistributed from the consumer to the seller.

—The large branches of the tree are symbolic of the different industries. Each of the large branches is supported by its related root system.

—The smaller branches that come off the large branches are symbolic of the supporting businesses that support the large industries. For example, one large branch may be the Auto industry. The smaller branches coming off that would symbolize businesses such as car dealerships, parts stores, gas stations, etc.

—The leaves of the tree are symbolic of the net profits after the operational costs are paid; after the company has invested in its own growth and paid off shareholders and investors.

Now some of the leaves can get bagged up and stored as assets, but a fair amount of the leaves should make it back down to the soil to fertilize the tree, to fertilize the consumer, and to fertilize the economy. And how do we get some of the leaves (net profits) back down to the soil (consumer)? We accomplish that through levying taxes and creating social programs.

That is the structure of Oak Tree Economics: it is a system that feeds itself for growth and sustainability. I know it may sound like it can't be that simple, but maybe it can be. Why can't we have a system that puts more money in the hands of the people who will spend it?

Give people the ability to acquire enough currency to be able to buy products and services. Every principle that is structured in the foundation of Capitalism needs to bring that to fruition.

I know it is a little more complicated than that. If we are going to build an economic system that works for everyone, it will be important that we understand what the two worst characteristics of Free Market Capitalism are and to fix them under this new system. The two worst problems we have with Free Market Capitalism are that the system doesn't care about poor people or the future. Poor people don't have the means to contribute to others gaining wealth, and the future is of no concern because profit statements are based on daily receipts.

Alan Jackson wrote a great song about the perils of a Free Market System; the song is called "Little Man." In the song he sings about how Big Business has replaced the independent business owners that built America. It was in the time of the independent business owner that Free Market Capitalism worked for America. Now we are in the age of Big Business, and the founding principles of Free Market Competition no longer exist. Big Business has little competition, they own the supply chains or own the delivery mechanisms, which makes it very difficult for any startup to compete.

Another one of the issues with a Free-Market System is that wealth equals power, and power equals control. And as time passes and wealth is being accumulated in large sums by relatively few individuals or major corporations, it is those people and those corporations that control the economy and do it for their own benefit. And who can blame them for that? I can't. If the economic system is set up without guardrails in place to protect the consumer and the taxpayer, you can't expect the people with power and control to vote against their own best interests. So, it is important to have some guardrails in place in the economy to keep the economy on a course to be fair and equitable.

Now let's be clear: I am not against Big Business controlling markets; that train has left the station, and there is no going back, and that's fine. We need an economic structure that moves us forward from where we are, not backward. But we are going to have to make big changes to how we manage certain industries.

An unregulated Free Market/Big Business system is self-suffocating and unsustainable. The money flows to the top and stays there, or it makes its way to foreign banks for safekeeping. When all that capital is taken out of the economy, growth slows down and that makes it hard for those at the bottom to be able to afford to buy products or services. Because when growth slows down, the cost of living goes up. Profit margin budgets are based on increases that have to be met, and Big Business Capitalism doesn't care about the poor or the future, so the cost of goods goes up and the cost of living goes up.

Oak Tree Economics will be sustainable because of the redistribution of wealth. Remember, Capitalism is based on the redistribution of wealth from the consumer to the business owner. Redistribution of wealth has never been a bad thing. Capitalism depends on it. Oak Tree Economics will have steady growth through the redistribution of some of the earnings back to the consumer in the form of tax relief and social programs. Tax relief will lower the bar on what a living wage is. A living wage is the minimum income necessary for a worker to meet their basic needs of food, shelter, clothing, and healthcare. If we can lower the bar on what a living wage is and slowly increase what is the minimum wage then we can get to a system where you can work hard and earn enough currency to participate in the economy at a high level. A high level not being measured by a dollar amount but instead being measured by the amount of purchases a consumer can make beyond what would be meeting their basic needs.

I know when people talk about the redistribution of wealth, they think of welfare programs and hand-outs. They talk about punishing the rich with taxes and using tax revenue to pay for programs for the poor. They will say redistributing wealth through taxes to the poor is Socialism. Social programs that lower the bar to what is a living wage are programs necessary to the success of Capitalism; they are not Socialist programs. They are Capitalist programs because they give a low-wage worker the means to participate in the economy beyond just meeting their basic needs.

Types of programs other than welfare programs need to be in place to help low-income workers and those individuals who are unable to work to be able to participate in the economy at the highest level they can. That is what fuels an economy and keeps it growing. I do not believe recessions are inevitable or necessary. Recessions occur in an economy because the mechanisms traditionally used to float or fuel the economy are not sustainable. The traditional mechanisms, such as Government spending and extending credit or tax cuts for corporations, are not sustainable and, used in the long term, are detrimental to the growth of the economy.

"Why should hardworking people have to give up the money they earned and have it given to people who are too lazy to work?" That is a fair question when it is talked about as a singular issue unrelated to any other part of a functioning economy. But let's remember that all economic policies need to be rooted in the goal of keeping as many people contributing to the economy as possible. We cannot set policy catering to an exception and not set policy that manages the rule. The fact that a small percentage of people are too lazy to work should not influence how we manage and regulate our economy. We need to govern by managing the rule that most people want to work hard and get ahead. I wonder why no one asks a question like this: "Why shouldn't large multinational corporations have to give up some of their profits to support the working poor and fertilize the economy?" The bottom line is we need to get the excess leaves of an Oak Tree Economy back down to the consumer to spend and fuel the economy. Let's not confuse hardworking people and Big Business as one and the same. We are going to ask Big Business to pay more in taxes to support the economy they are profiting from. It doesn't make sense to allow Big Business to drag down the economy and milk it for every penny they can get out of it. It puts the economy in a fragile position because many hardworking people end up living paycheck to paycheck. Living paycheck to paycheck limits how often they can participate in the economy beyond meeting their basic needs.

Hopefully you will be able to follow me as I try to explain this in simple terms. It is not unrealistic that we can make more money paying more in taxes. If we are willing to pay more in taxes to lower the bar on what is a living wage, we can increase the number of purchases that a lower or middle-class worker can make beyond paying for their basic needs. Follow me as I explain this using basic numbers. A company makes 100 dollars and pays 20 percent in taxes, netting them 80 dollars. Their tax rate goes up to 25 percent, but because their additional tax dollars are used to lower the bar on the living wage giving the consumer more money to spend, their gross sales increase by a modest 10 percent to 110 dollars. 110 dollars minus 25 percent in taxes nets them 82.50 in profits, a 3 percent increase in net profits. Businesses need to understand they are in business to make money and not save money. There is a saying that is so true in its underlying analysis, let me paraphrase it, "Companies often spend dollars trying to save quarters."

We are going to get into what I believe are the downfalls of our present economic system and how we can correct those by putting in some guardrails to keep us on track to a sustainable economy.

Our biggest problem is our present Tax Code. One of the pitfalls as it pertains to our Tax Code is the fact that those people with the most wealth are the people with the most control and power. And why would they shift the tax burden onto themselves and not keep it where it is; on the backs of the hardworking American who is trying to get by? I would never expect someone with great wealth to support a political candidate that would raise their tax burden. We can't expect that to happen. But what if that candidate was in favor of Oak Tree Economics, and even though the tax burden on the earnings of big business would go up, they wouldn't mind because their revenues and profits would go up as well? Revenues and profits would grow due to the sustained growth of an economy with a solid foundation. The Tax Code needs to be set up on a progressive scale: the more you make, the more you pay. The reason for that is the cause and effect, whether it is directly or indirectly, that the more money people make, it has the effect of raising the bar for what is a living wage in America. Major Corporations will pay the most. Major Corporations have altered the playing field the most by eliminating competition.

Corporations use motor freight to move products and motor freight causes the most wear and tear on the infrastructure in America. So why does the infrastructure bill fall on the backs of the average American through State and Local bonds paid for by State and Local taxes? I know there are Federal matching funds available and that does help. The infrastructure in America shouldn't be crumbling so major corporations can make thousands of millions of dollars per quarter. The Federal Government should be collecting enough in taxes to pay for the infrastructure improvements needed in this country; it should not fall on the States to pay. States have to pass it down to the average American to pay for. The Tax Code needs to adequately fund the Federal Government to maintain a sustainable economy.

The Guardrails needed for the tax code to maintain a sustainable economy need to do two things. First, the tax code needs to adequately fund the services provided by the Government and fund the Government so that it can care for its citizens in times of crisis, such as hurricanes, tornados, and pandemics. Second, the tax code needs to be set with limits to how much it can be adjusted or manipulated by different Administrations. We cannot have a President with business interests cutting the corporate tax code to benefit himself or his donors. That results in two things: it shifts the tax burden to the lower and middle-class workers at the State level and underfunds the programs meant to fuel the economy. I know some of you would say the Constitution protects that from happening. And it does when it is enforced. But a President is supposed to divest from his business interests before taking office, but we know now that doesn't always happen. And if members of Congress refuse to enforce the Constitution, what's in the Constitution doesn't matter. We need guardrails in place to ensure we have an economy that works for everyone.

Economic recessions are another downfall and are inevitable under our present economic system. Fast growth in GDP due to the government's procurement of goods leads to an economy built on a soft foundation. What happens when Government spending is forced to slow down? The economy slows down as well. Workers are laid off. Fewer workers mean less spending. Less spending means more workers are laid off. We do not want an economic system that thinks recessions are an unavoidable consequence. They are not. Think of an economy as a long-distance runner. They run too fast and then they have to slow down and walk. Or they can run at a good pace and moderately vary their speed but never have to slow down and walk. That is the premise of Oak Tree Economics, to retain a steady pace of growth. Oak Tree Economics is concerned about the future…and the poor. The poor people in America and around the world are the largest group of consumers with the largest potential for economic growth. Poor people, including the working poor, will spend any additional capital they are given. They will spend it trying to live a middle-class lifestyle. Why wouldn't an economy want them to have as much extra money as possible? The guardrail to avoid a recession is an economic foundation based on steady growth in the purchasing power of the poor.

Another downfall brought on by our present economic system is that the rate of America's population growth has dwindled. It is too expensive to have a large family, so the rate of growth of our workforce has dwindled as well. We have been taught to fear immigrants for being from somewhere else and not born here. So, population growth through immigration has slowed as well. The lack of an unemployed, employable workforce in America is a huge problem. 3.5 percent unemployment is way too low. The American dream is dead at that number. If you want to start a business and need 10–15 people with certain skills, good luck finding them when the unemployment rate is that low. What if you wanted to open a restaurant and need 30–40 employees? Where can you find them? They are already working, and you have to lure them away from their current job. Many people would say that is a good thing because now it starts a wage war, and wages go up. That is not the case. Businesses have a ceiling on what they can pay employees. Busy businesses close because of the lack of available employees. But this workforce problem is easily solved under Oak Tree Economics. Give hardworking people the means to pay for their basic needs and have extra money, and they will have larger families, and our workforce will have steady growth.

Immigration policies need to be set with the intent to manage the number of workers in the workforce. Immigration policies cannot be based on the fear of immigration. Immigration policies need to be flexible so they can be reactive to the needs of our workforce. The more workers we need, the more people we immigrate. The fewer workers we need, the more we reduce immigration. Immigration policy in America must be designed as a valve that can be adjusted and not a policy with a set number.

When it comes to immigration, what are the answers to the questions of Who, Why, and When? I am a firm believer in the immigration of families. Immigrant parents who love their children and immigrant children who love their parents, in my mind, are the best types of immigrants. A workforce rooted in family values is a solid foundation for a society grounded in morals and decency.

The guardrail we will need to have in place to best manage the growth of the workforce and the quality of the unemployed worker is an immigration policy that prioritizes immigrating families. And that includes immigrating family members of people already here in America. Two of the most important ingredients to a dynamic economy are having enough unemployed employable workers and to have a growing number of consumers who can participate in the economy at the highest level they can. The American Dream depends on both of those ideals.

A big part of the American Dream is to be able to work hard and provide for yourself and your family. Then, when you need to retire for any number of reasons, you should be able to collect enough Social Security to help sustain a decent quality of life. In order to fund Social Security, we need workers to pay into the program. That needs to be another consideration to how much we open the valve of immigration and increase our workforce. Not everyone can be the owner of a successful business and not need Social Security. Not everyone can be a successful doctor or lawyer and not need Social Security. But everyone who works hard to contribute to America's workforce and contributes to America's success should be rewarded with the means to retire and pay their bills when that time comes.

Once we have the guardrails in place to adequately fund the Government, to avoid recessions and to manage the size and growth of our workforce, then we can build on those guardrails with programs to lower the bar on what is a living wage. These programs will nourish the economy by giving a hardworking single person or married couple the ability to pay for their basic needs of food, shelter, clothing and healthcare and still have money left over to participate in the economy at the highest level they can. I cannot stress enough the importance that individuals or couples have the ability to work hard, 40–50 hours a week per person, and be able to make ends meet. When a young person works 50–60 hours a week and cannot make ends meet and they have no family who can help them, it is deflating to their spirit and soul. It is that kind of situation that can lead to alcohol and drug abuse. Not being able to make ends meet fuels a lack of self-esteem and self-worth in a person. When a person lacks a feeling of self-worth, it is very easy to fall into a cycle of drug and alcohol abuse. May even lead to feelings of suicide. If someone has the ability to work hard and get by and be able to enjoy the fruits of their hard work, then they are much less likely to fall into the trap of addiction and depression. And what I mean by working hard is not defined by having a college degree or starting a business; it includes people working hard at low-paying hourly jobs. Those low-paying jobs are essential to America's economy running smoothly. People need to be rewarded for taking those essential low-paying jobs. And the reward should be the ability to afford to have a family. A beautiful gift we could give back to God would be to give a person the ability to love, care for and provide for a family.

Now let's talk about some policies and programs that can achieve what we have set out to do. We want to have an economy that works for everyone. An economy where a low wage family can make ends meet and have some extra money to participate in the economy at the highest level they can.

The Food Stamp program is a great place to start. We need to increase the amount of people who qualify for food stamps by raising the income threshold for eligibility. And we need to raise the dollar amount of benefits for families. The cost of groceries has risen so fast, the level of benefits hasn't caught up. If we are to have an economy that works for everyone, we have to lower what is considered a livable wage by supplementing that wage with basic needs such as food. Remember our goal is to achieve an economy that fuels itself by having as many people participate in the economy at the highest level they can.

Another program adjustment that needs to be made is to adjust the earned income tax credit and make the benefit larger. And we need to lower federal income taxes being withheld on low-wage individuals and replace that tax revenue with higher taxes on those corporations that raise the standard of a living wage.

We need to help hardworking, low-wage workers afford daycare. Low-wage workers should be able to have larger families and get ahead. Our economy depends on it for steady growth. I have a way we can do that.

The cost of housing is one of the most expensive needs for a family. How do we bring the cost of housing down for low-income earners? I don't believe in rent control. Telling someone they can't charge what their rent is worth isn't fair to the landlord. It is the shortage of housing that drives up the cost of rents or homes. The cost of housing is breaking the backs of low-wage families before they even get going. One of the best and most effective ways to lower the bar for what is a living wage is to lower the cost of housing.

How do we help families afford housing and daycare? We build low-wage housing complexes; built and owned by the Federal Government.

These types of housing complexes will be self-sufficient and a revenue stream for the Government because renters will have their rent deducted from their paychecks weekly or bi-weekly. In the event they lose their job and are in between jobs for a short period of time, they would have their rent deducted from their unemployment check. Daycare would be provided within the housing complex. We would have affordable rent and daycare available for low-income wage earners and a revenue stream for the Government, lowering the tax burden for providing aid to the working poor.

These complexes would be different from housing projects that are neglected and crime-ridden. A lot of housing projects are brought down by the residents that can't work or make ends meet and turn to drugs and crime as a way to self-medicate and have some income.

The low-wage housing complexes would be made safe and crime-free by having only low-wage workers eligible for housing. Each complex would be deemed to be Federal property and any crime committed within the property boundaries of the complex would be considered a Federal crime. Each complex would have its own Federal Law enforcement agency on site to provide a safe environment for low-wage families to raise their children. They could raise the next generation of workers in a safe environment.

Low-wage workers would be hired to maintain the upkeep on the complexes. Residents would be encouraged to take pride and maintain the inside of their own residences. The idea of giving residents a sense of ownership in their living quarters means they are more likely to promote a healthy community that frowns upon and reports bad behavior and crime.

These complexes would promote economic growth for the areas chosen for development. Economic growth in the form of gas stations, restaurants, quick-care medical facilities, etc. I would think these types of complexes would be very beneficial to rebuilding our manufacturing sector and reducing our dependence on products from overseas. We could target areas in the country that have been economically depressed and abandoned by seeding them with industrial development? I would think the Federal Government could target segments of products that we are dependent on from other countries and begin to build them in America. Hospital supplies for example. If there is one thing we have learned from dealing with a pandemic, it is foolish to be dependent on foreign countries for our medical supplies. Even if we have to have the Government manufacture the supplies that may not be profitable for the private sector to manufacture. That would give us a great way to seed some depressed areas in America and rebuild America from the middle of the Country, out.

Another revenue stream for the public sector that would advance the quality of life and the economy would be a nationwide Wi-Fi network owned by the Government. I hate to say it but enough is enough with Communication companies saying they can't extend Broadband to every corner of every State because the return on investment doesn't justify the expansion. The Government can make it a low-cost network affordable for all income levels. That is going to create a revenue stream for the Government to help keep State taxes down.

If there is one thing, we have learned from this most recent pandemic is our economy depends on nationwide broadband, so employees can work from home if need be. Our education system depends on nationwide broadband to allow our kids to learn from home if need be. To allow communication companies to claim they can't afford to expand coverage is ridiculous. We give these companies two choices: be bought out by the Federal Government or just simply be replaced. It is time for broadband to be a public utility.

With an economy as big as the economy of the United States, there is no reason why the Government has to rely on taxes and fees as its only source of revenue. A great way to keep taxes down and services up is to have the Government take in revenue from low-income housing and broadband services. Two things every American need and two things that can really fund the programs needed to support low-wage workers and keep the American Dream possible for everyone.

Oak Tree Economics is very closely related to demand-side economics. But where it differs from demand-side economics is that I do not believe in the need for the Government to come in from time to time to float the economy with Government spending. If the workforce is maintained at the proper levels where there are enough employable people who are unemployed, then the economy can grow, and start-ups can find workers to work. When the workforce grows, that means more workers are out there participating in the economy at the highest level they can. They have enough currency to buy products and services over and above meeting their basic needs. And that spurs even more growth and alleviates the need for the Government to float the economy.

I know I have laid out some big ideas for creating an economy that works for everyone. If we are to achieve that goal, then we must go big or just continue to struggle and flounder in mediocrity. The biggest ideas are yet to come. I have big plans for changes to healthcare and education. The changes to healthcare are directly related to helping low-income workers participate in the economy at the highest level they can. The changes to education are directly related to maintaining and growing an effective workforce. We need to understand that big problems need big solutions.

We can make big changes and start down a course to making the American economy a shining star on the hill. Americans can show the world how Democracy is working for the benefit of all people: Americans, American immigrants, and people worldwide.

HEALTHCARE

Let's be civilized; let's care for our fellow human beings, as the God I believe in would expect that from us. Food, shelter, clothing and healthcare are the four basic needs we all need to live healthy, productive lives.

Why do we struggle with the cost of healthcare in this country? The United States spends nearly twice as much as other wealthy countries on healthcare, and we barely rate in the top ten for results and effectiveness. We are not getting our money's worth; there are other countries that spend half as much and get better results. Imagine America spending half as much and getting better results. Why can't the United States of America figure it out? If other countries can do it, I think we can figure it out. I think the conversion is less complicated than people think.

The healthcare system needs to be for-profit. Companies need to have the incentive to further research and develop new technology and treatments. But it is another thing for our healthcare system to be publicly traded on the stock market. Companies that are publicly traded are driven to achieve increases in profits year after year. These companies are often run by individuals that have compensation packages based on incentives to increase profits and return dividends to shareholders. These increases in profits and dividends are incentivized year after year after year. And we know in order to achieve those goals, the companies need to raise more revenue and control expenses. Healthcare companies are incentivized to raise the price of their products or services and lower the amount of revenue paid out. That is how we end up paying twice as much as other countries and having poorer results to show for it.

So how do we change a system that is so vast and so out of control when it comes to the cost per patient? The answer is slowly. I don't think the general public wants to see any radical new takeover of the healthcare system all at once. However, I do believe the general public would like to see changes that would lower costs and increase accessibility to affordable healthcare for all. We have all heard that sentiment before or something like it. But how do we really do it instead of just talking about it?

Let's put together a simple road map with some significant changes that will move us forward in a better direction. We know change can be scary, especially for something as important and personal as healthcare. But it needs to be done and we need to be brave and confident in our actions.

The pushback will be fierce and predictably obvious. The companies making big gains in profits won't want to change their ways. People will call these changes an un-American takeover of a privately owned industry. They will talk about how inept and inefficient the Federal government is. They will say it will lead to a rationing of healthcare and long waits for service and appointments. They will talk about the failures of other countries and their healthcare systems. But the one thing we do know is that out of failure comes success. There are very few, if any, great achievements that weren't born out of failures along the way. And no great achievements are ever accomplished through the fear of failure. Failure and mistakes are the stepping stones to success. Let's try to avoid as many mistakes and pitfalls as we can. And let's learn from the mistakes we make and move ourselves closer to what we are trying to achieve: affordable healthcare for all.

The first thing we are going to do is have the Federal Government buy out the insurance industry. Having the healthcare insurance industry publicly traded for profit is about as foolish a thing as I have ever seen. The industry right now is publicly traded and motivated to increase profits and reduce payouts. That means premiums go up and coverage goes down.

The insurance industry handles Medicare claims for the government; why don't we centralize the industry under one umbrella? We take over the insurance companies we have now, buy out their shareholders, and regionalize them. We divide up the country into regions and have the different groups of insurance companies manage their portfolios in their regions of the country. The insurance companies will be overseen by an insurance commission charged with oversight, compliance, and setting rates. This way no one working in the insurance industry gets laid off, and no one loses their job over a consolidation of an industry. The health insurance industry would not be consolidated: the industry would be divided up and groups of insurance companies put together to cover an area of the country with the ability to take on the expanded coverage for those without coverage right now.

The health insurance industry makes billions of dollars in net profits. And it is motivated to make billions more. Instead of the insurance companies paying billions to shareholders, we can take that revenue and lower the premiums for health insurance.

The second thing we do is start to build hospitals in underserved communities. It is important before we expand healthcare coverage to everyone that our system is big enough to handle the volume. We don't have to be burdened with long waiting periods to be seen or have healthcare rationed to only those who can afford it. We build a system large enough to function efficiently. Hospitals are like aircraft carriers: they need a fleet of facilities around them. Good paying jobs with benefits for individuals of all backgrounds. Building hospitals in underserved communities is a pathway out of poverty for many individuals in those areas. Hospitals hire individuals from all backgrounds, from brain surgeons to housekeepers. They hire people with Ph.ds, and they hire high school dropouts. Even better than that, building hospitals in underserved areas will give its residents employment opportunities as an alternative choice to joining gangs or using drugs. I believe that drug use is fueled by the depression that comes from trying to work hard just to find out that as hard as you work to make ends meet, you still can't get by. By giving the residents in underserved areas, a choice where they can be successful and get ahead, or they can be addicted and dependent, I believe more and more of them will choose a vehicle to success.

I know some hospital groups are held by a publicly traded management company. I do not believe we will have to buy out the shareholders of hospitals. As the government begins to build hospitals and expand the healthcare system, other hospital groups will want to fall in line to stay in public favor and stay afloat. At that point private hospitals can stay profitable without needing to be profit centers.

The third thing we need to do is set up a system that shares the cost. If everyone is given the ability to benefit from the system, then everyone needs to contribute. Individuals will pay through deductions in their payroll checks, deductions in their welfare checks, deductions in their food stamp assistance, or when they file a tax return on their earnings. Everyone needs to feel the burden of the cost and take ownership of paying for their own healthcare benefits, even if it's only in some small way. Employers will have to pay a flat rate amount per employee. This accomplishes the most important aspect of any successful healthcare system, and that is that everyone chips in. Right now, you don't have to pay a dime into the system. And when you have to go to the hospital, you will be treated, stabilized, and released with instructions to see a doctor for a follow-up. Which you may or may not do. You will probably get a hospital bill that you may or may not pay. When someone doesn't pay their bill, the cost is passed onto those who do pay. At the end of the year, the hospital has a certain amount of costs for providing service to patients who can pay and patients who can't, and those patients who can pay have to be charged enough to cover the costs for those who can't pay.

That will not be the case under this new system, as everyone pays in. I know one of you will come up with an example of how someone can avoid paying in by not declaring any income, earnings, or by not receiving any assistance from the State. Spouses who don't need to work will fall into this loophole. But we can capture most of those spouses when they file a tax return under the status of married and add a second contribution for the spouse on the tax return. As long as we can get 99 percent of the people and 99 percent of businesses contributing to the costs of healthcare, we can lower premiums and increase access to most everyone.

In 2020, 28 million Americans did not have health insurance at any point during the year. In 2018, 88 percent of employers with 500 employees offered health care as a benefit, 83 percent of employers with 100–500 employees offered health care as a benefit, and 55 percent of employers with less than 100 employees offered health care benefits to their employees. In 2020, there were over 31 million businesses in America. Which means there are millions of businesses not offering health care benefits to their employees and not paying into the health care system by subsidizing their employees' health insurance premiums. Under this new system, every business will be required to pay into the healthcare system on a per-employee basis, and that amount will be kept as low as possible. For example, if we add 10 million businesses paying into the system, and they have 30 employees each and pay 50 dollars a month per employee, then that raises an additional 180 billion in revenue per year. I know the numbers will need to be tweaked, and we may need a sliding scale where very small businesses pay less per employee and larger, more profitable corporations pay more per employee. I am confident we can lower the cost of healthcare for most Americans and probably lower the costs for most businesses that offer healthcare benefits right now.

Let's think about the importance of revamping our healthcare system. We spend the highest proportion of our GDP on healthcare when compared to Australia, Canada, France, Germany, the Netherlands, New Zealand, Norway, Sweden, Switzerland, and the United Kingdom. The performance rating of our healthcare system is dead last among those countries, and we are well below the next country above us. I mean well below, to the point of being shameful. Why can't we fix it, why haven't we fixed it?

The first reason is obvious: our healthcare system is a system for profit. Just about every aspect of our private healthcare system is owned by a publicly traded company. Publicly traded companies are pressured and geared for increases in profits, not geared for lowering the costs for consumers and not geared for better outcomes for patients.

The second reason we haven't fixed our healthcare system is the fear that there won't be enough healthcare to go around. How many times have you heard that universal healthcare is a socialist program and will lead to the rationing of healthcare? Then they go on to talk about other countries that have universal healthcare and the issues they have. If you boil down what they are saying, it boils down to this: "I can afford healthcare, and I don't care about those fellow Americans who can't because giving them healthcare may interfere with my ability to get healthcare when I need it." It doesn't matter to them that fellow Americans are in need of healthcare now but can't afford it. They would rather those Americans go without the healthcare they need today because of the fear they won't be able to get the healthcare they may need in the future. It boils down to a disdain for the poor.

I believe in Jesus. I believe he was one of the many prophets sent to teach us the ways of God and the expectations that God has for us. I believe Jesus washed the feet of his disciples as a teaching moment for all of us and he would want us to wash the feet of the poor and care for them.

I truly believe if we take these three steps and make these important investments, we can accomplish our goals. Let's review the three steps we need to take.

The first step is to take over and buy out the Health Insurance industry, taking it from a publicly traded for-profit industry and making it into a non-profit claim management industry.

The second step is to build a government-owned network of hospitals to handle the additional demand for healthcare to serve all Americans. Built in a manner to accent existing hospital networks, by being built in underserved areas that are not profitable enough to warrant private investment under today's expectations.

The third step is to make sure everyone is paying into the system, both individuals and businesses—everyone pays in. This will lower the costs for everyone. Why should the people who have insurance pick up the hospital bills of those who don't have insurance?

That is how we begin to lower the amount of money we spend as a country on healthcare and how we improve our results for the money we do spend. Let's not forget to mention the amount of extra money we spend on healthcare because we have a high percentage of the population with comorbidities that go undiagnosed or are under-treated until they end up in a state of emergency and go to a hospital. Prevention and early treatment of illnesses will dramatically lower our cost per patient over the life of the individual.

We can start on a course to make America a healthier nation with a healthier population; so we live better lives and spend less money per patient along the way.

EDUCATION

One of the key values we hold dear in this country, and rightfully so, is the right for every child to receive a good education. I believe in public education, and I believe we can do it right and be effective. What is the purpose of educating our children? The purpose is not to make them great thinkers, even though we need and love those who do become great thinkers. The purpose is not to turn them into Jeopardy champions full of facts and figures. The purpose is to prepare them to be good citizens of the United States of America. The purpose is to educate them in history, science, math, social studies, and so much more. And yes…to prepare them for the workforce.

We need to teach our children how to think and not what to think. We need to give them factual information and let them decide how they feel about an issue. We need to teach our children where to find factual information and to recognize misinformation that is presented in the format of being factual.

I am not in favor of public funding for charter schools. I do not believe tax dollars should be spent on education for profit or education of a certain ideology. If someone wants to send their child to a private school, that is great. They can pay for their child to go to a private school and still pay their taxes toward funding public education. Tax dollars are to be spent only on public schools, so every child can have a chance to receive a good education. There are a lot of people who would say, "Well how is that working for us now? A lot of schools are failing our children," and yes, that is true. But what is the reason for that? Is it us that are failing our schools, so our schools are, in turn, failing their students?

There are a lot of public schools that are doing great things by implementing ideas that would be described as outside the box. For example, one day I was listening to NPR in my car as I was doing my sales route, and a principal from a high school in the south serving an underprivileged area was talking about how he was able to increase the attendance at the school. He was able to increase attendance by providing laundry machines and toiletries to the students who needed them. It is hard enough being a teenager these days, but trying to attend school in dirty clothes, not being bathed, and not smelling fresh is not possible. Once the school provided time in the afternoon so kids could do their laundry, have a safe place to hang out, and gain a feeling of self-respect, they began to see a significant rise in attendance. Children who were falling through the cracks of society were given a vehicle to rise up. If you give a homeless child or an impoverished child a means to succeed, they will take it if they can see it for what it is. And then there are people, and I mean lots of people, who will say we can't provide all that for children, it would cost too much. Yet we know the truth; it costs us too much not to educate our children. And what would be the motivation of an adult to say it costs too much to provide some basic needs to a child so they would be able to attend school? Is it because they don't care about the poor because the poor can't contribute to their success? Is it because of greed?

Let's be realistic and truthful about education: there is a tremendous movement to hijack the education system. There is a narrative out there that public schools are trying to indoctrinate our children by telling them lies and teaching them to think a certain way. Are there circumstances where certain teachers have been caught doing just that, lying to their students to get them to think a certain way? I am sure there are, but they are rare. We cannot govern or educate our children by catering to an exception. We need to correct the teachers who are not presenting the curriculum in the proper manner. All in all, the public school system is doing a good job, and there are lots of terrific teachers helping our children to become well-educated citizens of the United States.

Not all schools need laundromats in the school, but some do. Let's provide those machines to the schools that need them. Not all schools need to be open into the evening to provide a safe space for children to hang out until one of their parents gets home, but some do. Let's give the schools the funding to tailor their resources to their needs. Not all schools need to have a nurse practitioner on staff to help with free medical care for a child, but some do. Let's make sure they have funding for that. We cannot make our schools the best they can be by painting regulations on them with a broad brush. We need to supply them with an extensive toolbox from which they can tailor their solutions to fit their needs.

How do we revamp our education system to better serve our country's children? How do we revamp our education system to better serve our need for a workforce? The issue we have right now is that many children graduate from high school not having a direction. Sure, they have a high school diploma, but they lack the skills needed to enter the job market. They need to further their education to be self-sufficient, whether that be an academic college or a vocational community college. Post-high school education costs a substantial amount of money. Not every high school graduate has the money or the means to borrow the money for a post-high school education. How do we fix that problem and have our children leave high school with enough skills to enter the workforce right away? Or have our children leave high school with a head start to seek further education no matter what their financial situation is?

I don't believe the idea of free community college will ever be able to pass Congress. But I do believe a structural change in the high school system can pass at the local level.

I believe we need to go to a five-year high school. We need to add a 13th grade. I know that sounds like a waste because what does another year add to a high school diploma? The answer is not much. I am not proposing a five-year high school diploma. As a matter of fact, I am proposing a three-year high school diploma. Let's be realistic: kids are learning so much more these days in their first three years of high school than we ever did in our four years of high school in the 60s, 70s, or 80s. I am proposing that a student can leave high school with a diploma after the 11th grade if they have the right number of credits that an enhanced 11th-grade education would require.

Now students who decide to stay in high school for a fourth and fifth year would then decide on which direction they would like to go. The two directions would be either a college-bound curriculum or a two-year vocational program.

A student choosing a college-bound curriculum would be able to choose a major and tailor their classes toward that major and complete their first two years of college in the 12th and 13th grades of high school. I know a lot of colleges probably wouldn't transfer those credits into their program and accept the student as a junior at their college. I get that. But we can have the State University system in each state recognize those credits and accept the student as a junior. A student might need to pick up an extra class or two depending on their choice of major. So, then a student would be coming out of high school with a two-year degree or with the first two years of a four-year degree completed. All of that achieved by attending high school for one more year. Now think about how much further ahead they would be. They would only need to pay tuition for their last two years of a four-year degree. The student would be much more likely to get financial aid and loans if it only takes two more years to complete their education.

Now what if a student chooses the direction of a vocational or trade curriculum for their 4th and 5th year of high school?

Have you tried to find a plumber or electrician to do a small project at your house? It is nearly impossible. They are all so busy with bigger, more lucrative projects. And it's not because the economy is booming so out of control; it is because there aren't enough of them. How is our economy going to expand if we don't have enough tradesmen to do the work? Think of all the other trades that we need to support our economy: car mechanics, HVAC technicians, sheetrock installers, roofers, culinary workers; the list can go on and on.

What if a student could go into a trade education program and, after 12th and 13th grade, come out having completed an apprenticeship program, being a certified car mechanic or a certified HVAC technician? Wouldn't that be a boost to our workforce and enable our economy to grow and thrive?

Now let's think of how we can get hands-on experience to our students and use that time to benefit the community in your area. These students, under the supervision of their teachers, who would be masters of their trade, could renovate municipal buildings, could build afford-able housing for low-income workers, and could partner with businesses in the area to acquire experience. The schools could actually create a revenue stream through this program and may be able to lower their tax burden on their local municipality. If done right, the amount of good that can be achieved through these programs is perpetual and endless.

What do we accomplish by going to a 5-year high school education program?

We allow students to achieve their goal of a high school diploma and enter the workforce at the age of 17. We enable students to acquire a 2-year college degree by adding one more year of high school. These 2-year degrees are transferable into the State University system lowering the cost of achieving a 4-year degree almost in half. Private colleges will have to determine how many of these credits they will choose to accept. If a student chooses to go to a private college, whether or not that col-lege accepts any transfer of credits doesn't really matter; the student will be that much further along in their ability to do the work and adjust to being away from home.

What about the issue of a student-athlete? They could leave after 3 or 4 years and go to a private college or university. Or they could leave after 5 years and be that much further ahead and still go onto a private college and play sports. A student-athlete could stay in high school, at-tend the trade program, and play sports through their 5th year. Yes, stu-dents get to play high school sports for 5 years if they choose to stay in school for that period of time. I don't see how we can get around that and I don't see an issue with it anyway. If anything, it will promote a stronger freshman sports program. Instead of having freshmen play at a JV or Varsity level, they can be mandated to play at the Freshman level. On the flip side, any 5th year student would have to play at the Varsity level and not play down at a JV level.

Instead of a child not seeing the benefit of staying in school, they will see that staying in school can provide a vehicle to enter the workforce with the ability to provide for themselves through meaningful employment. I would have to believe that would bring down the drug use and homelessness that is plaguing our society.

The purpose of a High School education has to be to prepare the vocational bound student to enter the workforce with the ability to be effective and self-sufficient.

The purpose of a High School education has to be to prepare the college-bound student with as many undergraduate credits they can achieve and lower the cost of achieving a four-year college degree or a master's degree in a certain field.

The purpose of a High School education needs to be that it provides a vehicle to successfully enter the workforce and to enter the workforce with the ability to be effective and self-sufficient.

We can set a course to where a public education can provide a path to success for children of all abilities.

CLIMATE CHANGE

I don't want to get into an argument about whether climate change is a man-made issue due to fossil fuel emissions. I don't want to argue about whether climate change is a part of a natural cycle of weather patterns. I don't want to argue about the ozone layer getting too thin to filter UV rays from the sun. Is that why the sun is feeling stronger, and sunburns seem to be more of an issue than when I was young? The science is established on the issue of climate change and those who don't want to believe the science will never believe the science. Let's move on from agreeing to disagree on the science of climate change. The younger generation has realized how futile it is to try and reason with some adults over the issue of climate change. The real issue with fossil fuels is they are running out. And once they are gone, they are gone.

The world uses oil, natural gas, and coal to help fuel its energy needs. They are used to create electricity, heat, and cool our homes. Fossil fuels are used to fuel our cars and power industry and manufacturing. The world uses 97 million barrels of oil per day to help fuel a large part of the world's energy needs. The world uses 10 billion cubic meters of natural gas per day to help fuel a part of the world's energy needs. Those are huge amounts of consumption every day, day after day. Natural gas and oil are by far the two largest sources of energy used to fuel the world's energy needs. When looking at those amounts of oil and natural gas that are consumed each and every day, it leads me to wonder how much oil and natural gas are left? I know it took the earth millions of years to form the oil and the natural gas we extract from the ground. So how much is left in the ground? What is a good estimate?

According to Worldometers.info and the United States Geological Society, the best estimate of how much proven oil reserves are left in the world and how long they will last, based on 2016 consumption levels, is about 50 years. And as hard as it may be for you to believe, it was just as hard for me to believe when I read it. They say there are undiscovered oil reserves out there as well. Should we really plan our future on what may be out there for oil reserves, or should we plan our future on what we know to be proven oil reserves?

Natural gas reserves are about the same, 50 years' worth. That means in about 50 years, the world will be out of oil and natural gas, which supplies almost 80 percent of the world's energy needs every day, day after day. That is a scary thought. We have less than 50 years to replace 97 million barrels of oil usage per day. We have less than 50 years to replace 10 billion cubic meters of natural gas usage per day. We better figure this out, starting now. Even if we have 100 years left in our reserves, it means we are still running out. We have figured out that fossil fuels are not good for our environment on the only planet we have. Yet for some reason, we are choosing to use every last drop of it. Why?

Whether you believe in climate change or not. Whether you believe climate change is a man-made phenomenon due to the greenhouse effects of burning fossil fuels, or it's not. None of that matters there isn't an endless amount of fossil fuels left in the world. We should start changing over to renewable energy.

All of you out there that want to deny the science of climate change can't deny the fact that we will be running out of fossil fuels someday. The business of energy will always be big revenue for big companies. What better source of big revenue is there other than renewable sources of energy at a global scale? Let's help the big oil companies make the transformation into being big renewable energy companies. Let's get it right this time; let's choose energy sources that work for us and the planet.

The forces of nature have always proven to be powerful. Let's find a way to harness that power then set it free to be harnessed again.

The benefits of moving away from fossil fuels sooner rather than later are tremendous. The atmosphere will have decades to start healing itself. The impact of catastrophic weather will begin to decrease. The impact of wildfires will be reduced. UV rays will begin to get filtered closer to the levels they used to be. Birds will begin to thrive again. Polar bears and penguins will have a place to live and all will be well with Mother Nature. I believe the atmosphere can and will begin to heal itself. The Bio-Systems of Mother Nature are powerful and resilient.

It's not hard to vote for people who want to save the Earth. It's not hard to vote out climate change deniers. It's not hard to vote out politicians holding onto fossil-based fuels that poison our environment.

It's not hard to do the right thing and start moving in the right direction.

It's not hard to set a course for a healthier planet.

RACE

Let's talk about Race. Let's talk about our differences in culture. Let's try to understand how human nature can drive our feelings of superiority over other Races. These feelings of superiority can be driven by what should be innocuous differences such as hair styles, clothing, fashion, and music genres.

Let's talk about the power of choice. Choices can change the way we treat each other. Choices can create peace and change the world.

Racism in America is a huge problem. It is a generational problem that will take generations to solve. I am very hopeful for our next generation that is in Middle School, High School, and College in the year 2024 to be the generation that turns the corner on racism in America and moves us in the right direction. The direction I believe God would want us to go in. The direction that God would have expected us to have taken a long time ago.

Evolution takes time. It takes generations to fundamentally change the hearts and minds of men and women. We cannot go from justifying lynching and segregation to equality in one or two generations. Unfortunately, as human beings, we are victims of our own human nature. We view ourselves as masters of our universe in real-time, but we are not. We think we can do anything, even accomplish social change based on reason and desire, but that is not true. We are reflections of what has been passed onto us by the experiences and attitudes of generations before us. We need to embrace the experiences and beliefs that our parents have passed on to us, whether they are right or wrong, and then take the recognition of that embrace and make better choices.

The best way to change the hearts and minds of men and women is to embrace how they got to where they are now, being tolerant of how they got there takes away the disdain you may feel for them and replaces it with acceptance. Human nature being what it is, if we are attacked for our beliefs, we tend to dig in and defend ourselves, making change and evolution more difficult. A lot of people were raised racist. They were told to fear people that are a different color than themselves. White people were taught to fear black people. Black people were taught to fear white people. We were taught to fear the Irish. We were taught to fear the Japanese. We were taught to fear Middle Easterners. Now we are being taught to fear Mexicans and Latinos. Is it me, or do we see a pattern here? Little children aren't born knowing the N-word. But they hear it and learn it. Young Adults read racist rants on their phones and choose to hate. We cannot ignore how easy it is to find the seeds of hate on the internet. And how easy it is to plant the seeds of hate in our own lives without even knowing it.

Free speech and hate speech are two different things. Art and pornography are two different things, and the Court said about telling the difference is that you'll know it when you see it. It's the same thing with free speech and hate speech, you can tell the difference. There is no justification for a legal right to threaten, intimidate, or insight violence against a sub-race to the Human race. We need to be better than that. It's ok for us to recognize our mistakes and correct them. We can be forgiven for believing what we were born to believe. We don't have to dig in our heels and defend what we were raised to believe. It doesn't mean anyone is at fault for living an ideal they were taught to believe in. It doesn't mean anyone is any better than someone else because they were raised not to hate. What all of that does mean is that we, as Human beings, can choose to be a better race, a better Human Race. Take away all we have been taught to fear and we can see we are all members of the same Race, the Human Race. We cannot have contempt for the people who hate, that only completes the cycle of hate. And breaking the cycle of hate must be our goal as it relates to racism.

We need to stop saying that different Races are equal. We are all different and unique. Our natural perception of all of us being equal is that we are all the same. Each Race has characteristics that have been passed onto them by the generations before them, and these characteristics are different from Race to Race. But if we are taught that we are all equal and therefore all the same, we will view our cultural differences with disdain. We will look at other Races with different cultures and say to ourselves, "I would never wear clothes like that or have a hairstyle like that. What are they thinking?" We need to embrace the cultural differences from Race to Race as a vehicle for growth. It is through embracing and understanding our cultural differences that those differences become less apparent and less annoying. A great example of that is gangster rap music. Me, being a white man in my sixties, I have never enjoyed the filthy, violent lyrics of gangster rap. I don't see the enjoyment of it. But I have two teenage basketball players who enjoy it, and I have learned to lose my disdain for it, tolerate it, and listen to it in the car with the kids. Let's stop trying to convince each other we are all equal because we are not. Let's try to convince each other we are all different and that's ok. It is ok to be different. And individuals who treat others with respect and dignity deserve to be treated the same.

People say the different races need to be equal in the eyes of the law. But we know that an unarmed person of color is much more likely to be killed by a law enforcement officer than an unarmed white person. Let me say that is not Just or Right. But we cannot expect law enforcement officers to treat all people equally. A police officer is a human being with a personal history and is the reflection of their upbringing with their parents and grandparents' attitudes and beliefs.

A police officer needs to treat each individual individually. Each individual has beliefs and attitudes that will present themselves in unique ways to a police officer. A person might be confrontational, or they might be respectful and considerate toward a police officer. Either way a police officer needs to know how to treat each person as an individual and be able to bring about the proper ending to their unique encounter.

Whether that be an arrest, a summons, or just a warning. No unarmed person deserves to be killed for having a broken taillight. No unarmed person deserves to be killed for passing a phony 20-dollar bill they may not have known to be counterfeit. No one deserves to be choked to death by a police officer for selling loose cigarettes on the street to support their wife and children.

Let's take a moment and talk about the Amy Cooper incident in Central Park. An incident where a woman falsely claimed a black man was threatening her and her dog. She had called the police, knowing they would believe her and arrest the black man because that is what happens to black people. They get arrested for crimes they never committed because there are people out there willing to lie to the police, knowing they will be believed over the word of the black man. But in this incident, the black man was recording her with his phone, and she was arrested for filing a false report. But these types of incidents are very common and often end with the black man being arrested for a crime they didn't commit. The black man in the Amy Cooper incident was lucky that the police officer who was there was willing to believe him and look at the video with an open mind, looking for the truth.

Let's look at the incident with Antone Austin, who wasn't so lucky. A black music producer who was detained and arrested while taking out his trash. The police were called to the house next door for a domestic violence dispute involving a white suspect. Instead of going to the right house, they chose to stop at Austin's house while he was taking out the trash and immediately tried to handcuff him, he resisted, claiming they had the wrong house and the wrong guy, but he was arrested for resisting arrest. The woman next door who made the call to the police came out and told the police they had the wrong house and the wrong guy. Austin was arrested anyway. And the police never made it to the right house next door to address the actual 911 call that was placed. He was lucky that he could afford to post the high bail that was set and was able to get out of jail. Most black men falsely arrested can't make bail and spend weeks or months in jail until their charges are dropped or they are falsely convicted. I was listening to NPR when the body cam video of this incident was released. NPR had a public defender on the segment as a guest, and the guest stated how she had defended hundreds of black men falsely accused of crimes they did not commit. Black men arrested by police officers who knew they were innocent or, at the very least, knew there wasn't enough evidence to make an arrest, yet they were arrested anyway. Incidents like this reverberate through the black community, creating fear and disdain toward police officers and the justice system.

A police officer needs to be trained on how to bring about the proper outcome when encountering different individuals. Understanding that people of color have been taught through experience to fear for their lives when encountering a law enforcement officer, even for the most innocuous offenses. Those fears are real and justified. An officer needs to understand their fear is justified and may cause them to be agitated and irrational. But, with the proper training, an officer can learn to ease the fear by remaining respectful and calm instead of being forceful and domineering. Respect cannot be achieved by dominating your potential adversary, it can only be earned by staying calm and justifying your actions. When a suspect realizes an officer has no choice but to arrest them, the arrest has a much better chance of not being a violent confrontation.

Trust me, I realize there may be circumstances that will justify killing an unarmed suspect. But if a law enforcement agency can do things Right, Fair, and Just most of the time, then people will understand when things go wrong and give them the benefit of the doubt when they kill an unarmed suspect due to unforeseen circumstances. That may lead to a day when emotions will stop boiling over into riots and hatred towards the police and government.

We want to teach our children that police officers are not the enemy. But we can only hope to achieve that if police officers don't act like our enemy. Police officers have a very stressful and difficult job. They put their lives on the line every day. And we need to appreciate that and give them all our respect and cooperation.

I have told my kids many times that doing the right thing is always the right thing to do. It may not be the most popular or easiest thing to do at the time, but in the end, when it's all over and the dust of chaos has settled, they can hold their head high.

Police officers have the same opportunity when it comes to policing themselves. The Blue Code of Silence has got to end. We find ourselves where we are because of it. The Blue Code of Silence perpetuates the attitude of them against us. Law Enforcement against the rest of us. That cycle of hate has got to end. There is no justification for crimes by law enforcement against civilians. There is no justification for false reports and cover-ups for crimes committed by law enforcement against civilians. Calling out your fellow officer for committing crimes is the right thing to do. Doing the right thing is always the right thing to do, no matter how unpopular or difficult it may seem at the time.

I believe police officers should get a paid working vacation, separate from the personal vacation time they have earned, to a summer camp with other law enforcement officers. This will give them an outlet to relieve the stress they have built up. It will give them a chance to enjoy all the activities of a lakeside camp. And I think the best benefit of all will be the opportunity to talk to and hang out with others who know what they have been going through. The fellow officers can share their experiences of success and failure with each other. It can be therapeutic to talk about your failures and realize it's ok to be human.

It is hard to talk about racism without talking about white supremacy and its influence on our lives. White Supremacy dates back to before the United States existed. It was the foundation for European expansion and colonization. The belief that the white race was superior and was meant to dominate all other races. It has been widely believed throughout history that the White Race was the chosen race by God and any actions to reaffirm that belief is justified by God to be his will. The God I believe in doesn't believe the white race is the chosen race. The God I believe in doesn't believe the white race is superior to all other races. The God I believe in believes we are all his children, no matter the color of our skin. White Supremacy and Racism have no place in the house of the Lord and no place in the palace of God. You have to ask yourself, "Why would people who claim to be followers of Christ be against teaching what racism is? Why would people be against shining light on the hatred that white supremacy promotes and acts upon?" People who choose to dim the light on the hatred of white supremacy and racism are white supremacist and racists themselves. You can't vote for a racist and not be a racist. You can't vote for a white supremacist and not be a white supremacist. What you can do is not vote for a racist or a white supremacist.

In America, we have a history of white supremacy over African Americans. In Europe, there is a history of white supremacy over Jews. In the Middle East, there is a history of white supremacy over Arabs. It is important to call attention to it wherever it exists. Hard to say it isn't the single biggest cause of violence around the world. People have the right to buy into the ideology. People have the right to think they are superior to other races. It is when their beliefs lead to hatred and violence toward others that it crosses the line of decency and acceptance. People also have the right to call them out when they cross the line. People don't have to vote for white supremacists. People don't have to vote for nazis. People don't have to vote for people who support leaders who choose to expand their borders without consequence because they feel they are entitled. There are many more people in the world who want peace so they can live a safe life than there are people who want war. Achieving peace around the world is not that difficult. Peace is nothing more than a choice to achieve it.

Let me solve the Israeli-Palestinian conflict in one long paragraph. Both sides need to show respect and compassion for the other side's history, with all its baggage. Palestinians need to turn in and punish anyone who commits violence or plans to commit violence against the Israelis. Israelis need to give back much of the land they have seized in this century, the last 20 or so years by simply having the people of Israel choose to move out and give these settlements back to the Palestinian people. The

Israeli Government needs to release the Palestinian prisoners being held without having committed a crime. They are being held indefinitely because they might commit a crime. The Israeli Government sweeps up hundreds of Palestinians at a time and holds them without any charges, isn't that hostage-taking? They need to release all of those hostages they call prisoners. Peace can be achieved by those who want it by showing justice toward the other side. By denouncing and removing the leaders who choose violence and expansion, a peaceful acceptance of each other as human beings and children of God will prevail. It will take the total unacceptance of violence and hatred toward the other side by the people of both sides. That is not very hard to achieve. That has got to be the will of God as we know it to be. And doing the right thing is the right thing to do. Peace can be a choice by the people of Israel and by the people of Palestine. They can choose war as a vehicle to prove they are full of hate, or they can choose peace by showing respect and compassion for the other side. The power of choice is amazing in what it can achieve.

What if Americans choose to accept our Racial differences in culture, experiences, and skin color? Wouldn't America be a better place to live? Why wouldn't we want America to be a better place for all Races to live?

We can set a course for Americans to come together and accept our cultural differences. We can set a course for all Races to be celebrated and respected.

GAY MARRIAGE

I was going to write this long chapter on how the Constitution of the United States allows for Gay Marriage and even protects the right for two people to marry under the religion they choose to recognize and believe in. But then, in the case of *Hodges vs. Obergefell*, the Supreme Court of the United States legalized Gay Marriage nationwide, not giving me much to write about.

Then I read the dissenting opinions to *Hodges vs. Obergefell* by Chief Justice Roberts and Antonin Scalia. Their biggest concern with the majority decision was that it took the issue away from the individual States, thus taking it away from the voters. They thought the Justices in the majority were legislating from the bench.

Roberts wrote, "Under the Constitution, judges have power to say what the law is, not what it should be." Ironically, I thought that is exactly what their job was, to tell us what the law should be as it pertains to the issue before them. Ruling one way or the other on an issue as it relates to the Constitution of the United States is their job. He goes on to say, "Our Constitution does not enact any one theory of marriage. The people of a State are free to expand marriage to include same-sex couples, or to retain the historic definition." That is a huge step to take: just because the word "marriage" is not defined or mentioned in the Constitution, then it must be a State issue? Whenever an issue is brought to the Supreme Court by petitioners who feel they have been wronged, it is the Supreme Court that decides under which Constitutional law or laws that have standing with regard to deciding the case. The Court can't say, "Sorry, the specific issue is not addressed in the Constitution, so we are unable to rule, even though there are broad sweeping Constitutional laws that the issue may fall under." I look at the Constitution as one big umbrella with many smaller umbrellas under it. And each of the smaller umbrellas represents a law that might pertain and be used to decide a case.

Antonin Scalia wrote in his dissent to *Hodges vs. Obergefell* (and this is Antonin Scalia in a nutshell), "So it is not of special importance to me what the law says about marriage. It is of overwhelming importance, however, who it is that rules me." On the issue of marriage, he doesn't care under which umbrella of laws the issue may fall under, he cares more about who is ruling on it, the Supreme Court or voters. He doesn't even care if the voters get it wrong as long as they are the ones deciding. I once heard him say in response to a follow-up question at a speaking engagement in front of law students during the Q&A session (I am paraphrasing here but this is pretty darn close), "I don't care what the law says, that's how I feel." Is he really the guy that is held up and revered for his legal mind? Sounds more like he is likely guilty of legislating from the bench with no regard for what the law says about an issue.

You have dissenting opinions totally ignoring the rule of law and what the Constitution says about the Gay Marriage issue, which easily settles the debate. Supreme Court Justices need to be men and women built of integrity and a desire to seek the truth. So, let's talk to the truth about what the Constitution says about Gay Marriage.

Let's establish a very important fact about marriage. Marriage in this modern era is a religious event. I know people want to define marriage as a legal union and a legal contract with religious overtones optional. But is that really what marriage is? I do understand there are legal benefits to being married, and couples need to sign legal documents declaring their consent to be married to each other. If we are to look at the history of marriage, it has not necessarily been a consensual agreement between a man and a woman.

Marriages started as arraignments between families to secure a better advantage. Earliest marriages were about 4300 years ago. They were not marriages for love and commitment. They were business arrangements aimed to secure a better standing in society.

The history of marriage is ugly. People will talk about the history of marriage as always having been between a man and a woman. How we need to stay with the tradition of marriage. Can we talk about what the tradition of marriage really was? It was an arrangement where the man virtually owned the woman. He could beat her, rape her, or murder her with impunity. Is that the traditional marriage we are trying to preserve and get back to?

Justice Roberts, in his dissent, goes on to say, "The people of a State are free to expand marriage to include same-sex couples, or to retain the historic definition." Are we really going to say States can have the right to define marriage in traditional terms based on ancient societal arrangements?

Roman Law allowed for men to beat, divorce, or murder their wives for dishonoring their husbands or threatening their family wealth. Is that the historical definition of marriage Justice Roberts is talking about?

It took women centuries to overcome the principles of coverture, the belief that a woman's legal status was owned by her father and then surrendered over to her husband at the time of marriage. The husband would then have all legal authority over his wife's affairs. Is that the historic definition that Justice Roberts wants to allow States to go back to if they so desire?

Let's talk about how the definition of marriage has changed over fairly recent times.

Wife beating was finally made illegal in the United States in 1920. So, did Justice Roberts mean the historical definition of marriage before 1920 or after 1920?

Interracial marriage bans were ended by the Supreme Court in 1967 in the case called, *Loving vs. Virginia*. Is Justice Robert's historical definition of marriage before 1967 or after 1967?

It was in 1974 when the Equal Credit Opportunity Act was passed, that gave women the right to seek credit on their own without a husband's signature. A woman was allowed to manage her own affairs without her husband's approval. Is Justice Robert's historical definition of marriage before 1974 or after 1974?

These are all very significant changes to the definition of marriage. It certainly appears that the definition of marriage has been evolving for centuries and has been evolving most significantly in the last 100 or so years as societal and economic opportunities have evolved for women.

To bring my point full circle, marriage is less about a civil legal union where the woman assumes the identity of the man and surrenders all her legal standing as an individual to him; now marriage is more of a religious ceremony with some tax benefits given to the married couple. A religious ceremony where two people profess their love for each other in front of the God they choose to believe in.

Most of the groups opposing Gay Marriage are religious-based groups. Which furthers the point that marriage these days is more about being a religious ceremony than a legal event protecting wealth and property or seeking an advantage in society.

These groups opposing Gay Marriage are known for spreading lies and misinformation about Gay tendencies and relationships. They often talk about how the Gay community is trying to recruit and convert children into being gay. A lot of their lies and misinformation revolve around sexual acts with children and pedophilia. Studies have determined that gay individuals are no more likely to have sex with children than heterosexual individuals.

It amazes me how people seem to talk about homosexuality in terms of sex and not intimacy. I have a friend of mine whose son has grown up to be gay, and my wife and I suspected he would be gay when he was very young. My wife and I have two daughters, and by the way he played with them, it was fairly obvious at a young age he would be gay. We never said anything, and then, when his son was in high school and came out as gay, my friend and his wife were devastated and upset.

My friend came to me and said a mutual friend told him to tell his son he could choose to be straight. We sat down and talked for a while.

I explained to him that being gay isn't a choice. Being gay is not about choosing who you are going to have sex with, it is about intimacy. Being gay is about who you can cuddle with, who you can kiss, whose arms you can lay in and fall asleep. I further told my friend that what our mutual friend was saying was that he himself could choose to be gay. He could choose to lie in another man's arms. We both laughed because we knew that our friend could never choose to be gay. My friend, whose son is gay, could never choose to be intimate with another man, and neither could I. It was from that day forward he accepted his son as a gay man. He understood what it means to be gay. He wanted his son to know love and acceptance. He wanted his son to be who he was born to be.

Let's see how Gay marriage relates to the law. Let's see if we can see how it is protected by the Constitution like I believe it is

Let's go into a County Clerk's office and watch two couples try and get a marriage license. The first couple is a heterosexual couple in their 30s. They have been together for 5 years and have been engaged for over a year and the big day is only a few weeks away. They belong to the church just down the road from the Town Hall and plan to get married in the church. They are told to come back the next day and pick up their marriage license. It will be ready then.

The second couple is a same-sex couple in their 40s. They have been together for over 10 years. They feel it is time for them to get married and share the benefits that married couples enjoy. They belong to the same church right down the street as the first couple and plan to get married in the church as well. There are thousands of churches representing several different religious denominations in America that would perform a same-sex marriage ceremony. These churches collectively have millions of parishioners, they have millions of Americans belonging to these churches in towns all across America. The second couple is told they cannot get a marriage license because they are a same-sex couple.

I am confused about how that is possible in America. You have two couples looking to get married in the same church by the same pastor and one couple is told that they can't because their State has banned them from getting married.

The 14th Amendment of the United States Constitution says in Section One: "No State shall make or enforce any law which shall abridge the privileges or immunities of citizens of the United States; nor shall any State deprive any person of life, liberty, or property, without due process of law; nor deny to any person within its jurisdiction the equal protection of the laws."

The First Amendment of the Bill of Rights of the United States Constitution protects a person's right to practice their religious beliefs; especially if those beliefs are mainstream and shared by many others. I am sure there are some religious beliefs, from devil worshipers, for example, that may not pass the legal test. But these two couples are so similar in the fact they live in the same town, worship at the same church, and want to profess their love to each other in front of the God both couples believe in. But because the legislators of their State chose to impose their religious beliefs onto the same-sex couple, the same-sex couple is denied the ability to get married. They are denied their right to practice their religion and are forced to live under the religion of others.

The 14th Amendment prohibits any State to make or enforce a law that abridges a right given to all citizens in the Bill of Rights in the Constitution. The First Amendment of the Constitution of the United States is a cornerstone of our protected freedoms in this country. The First Amendment protects the practice of Religion by like individuals.

Can we take a moment and look at who it is that is trying to ban same-sex marriages and why? I think it is pretty safe to say that it is religious groups that are trying to ban same-sex marriages because they do not believe that same-sex marriages are approved by the God they believe in. They believe that homosexuality is a sin on a personal level and allowing same-sex marriages is a sin on a societal level. I understand that living in a country that allows behavior that is against what they believe in and have been told by their preacher is a sin is hard to accept. But in America accepting another person's religious beliefs is what this country was founded on. We do not have to practice a religion someone else believes in, but we do have to respect their right to believe in it.

Gay Marriage is, without any doubt, a religious ceremony protected by the First Amendment. A religious ceremony accepted by millions of fellow parishioners in many different religions. The 14th Amendment further protects their right to get married by prohibiting any State from making or enforcing any law which attempts to override a citizen's protected freedom as stated in the Constitution of the United States.

I find it hard to understand how this could be an issue to be determined by the States, as claimed by Justice Roberts and Justice Scalia. It is virtually impossible to justify denying the second couple a marriage license based on their gender rather than granting them a marriage license based on their freedom to practice the religion they believe in. A religion with a religious ceremony that is accepted by millions of other Americans.

What is even harder to understand is how the present Supreme Court has stated they are open to revisiting the ruling that legalized Gay Marriage nationwide and making it a State-by-State issue. In the vein of Antonin Scalia, they don't care about what the law says; they care more about who is making the law.

We can set a course where different religious beliefs are tolerated and ceremonies are held privately by those who share those beliefs.

ABORTION

Let's take on the issue of abortion. A subject with no apparent compromise. A subject that brings out the deepest emotions of those who are passionate about the issue. An issue that is exploited to divide us and bring about anger and hatred between us.

I believe there is a compromise and a solution to this issue. It may not please everyone, but what compromise ever does? If we could come to a compromise on this issue, imagine how much of what divides us would be gone.

I am not going to explain and list what both sides believe in. I am not going to go into how everyone's religious beliefs play into their stance on the issue. That would probably solidify each person's position on the issue and make any compromise that much harder for us to achieve. To achieve compromise, it takes both sides to move off their perch and step toward each other and meet somewhere in the middle.

What does a compromise on abortion look like? It looks like a world with far fewer abortions being performed. It looks like a world with far fewer women dying from an ill-fated pregnancy. It looks like a world where young single women can choose to have a baby and know they will receive the support they need to keep the baby. It looks like a world where young women can choose to have a baby and choose to give it up for adoption, knowing the child will be well cared for. It looks like a world where a woman can choose to send the soul of a malformed fetus back to God to care for.

Let's look at what's in the compromise for the Pro-life movement:

- 3rd-trimester ban on elective abortions
- Universal healthcare for pregnant women; covering 100 percent of prenatal care; covering 100 percent of labor and delivery costs; covering 100 percent of postnatal care for the mother and the infant; covering 100 percent of quality-of-life procedures for the infant (i.e. a cleft lip or palate)
- Financial assistance to support a woman's desire to keep her baby and be able to work and still care for her child
- A quality State-run adoption agency for women who choose to give up their baby for adoption
- A well-funded foster care program for the children unable to be adopted

Every one of those bullet points will reduce the number of abortions in America. A woman will choose to have an abortion because they feel it is the right thing to do at the time. It won't be because they can't afford to have a child. It won't be because they don't have insurance. It won't be because they don't have family members to help with childcare. It won't be because they feel if they give up their child after birth that it won't be well cared for. Those are the main reasons why women have abortions, and they are all addressed in this compromise with the intent to lower the number of abortions.

Let's look at what's in this compromise for the Pro-choice movement:

- A woman can get an abortion throughout the first two trimesters of her pregnancy
- A woman can get an abortion in the third trimester of her pregnancy to save the woman's life
- A woman can get an abortion in the third trimester of her pregnancy if the fetus is not viable
- A woman can get an abortion to save her ability to get pregnant in the future

Every one of those bullet points keeps a woman's decision to have an abortion between her and her faith. Three of those bullet points keep the decision to have an abortion between the woman and her doctor. There are many complications that can arise during a pregnancy where a woman and her doctor need to weigh the risks of continuing the pregnancy and those decisions need to be made by them and them alone.

I want to talk a little bit about how a woman's choice to have an abortion can be a decision between her and her faith. It really isn't much of a stretch to have an abortion based on your religious beliefs.

I believe God has entrusted me and all humans with caring for this planet. I believe God expects us to care for and shepherd his creation, known as Mother Nature, so it stays as healthy and as viable as possible. I believe that overpopulating this planet with humans will cause the extinction of some of God's creatures and break the balance of nature. Are we, as humans, so arrogant to think our overpopulation is more important than the health and well-being of our one and only planet to live on?

I believe that God has given us the miracle of medicine not only to save lives but also to control our population. We have the ability to save lives, but do we have the foresight to control the population of human beings? If we overrun our planet, we will start wars over the need for resources. If we overrun our planet, we will destroy our atmosphere with toxic pollution. If we overrun our planet, we will forever break the balance of nature and ruin the quality of life for humans for generations to come and maybe forever.

It is time for Americans to understand a compromise is in our best interest. If you do not believe you should have an abortion, then don't have one. If you do not believe anyone should have an abortion, then believe in their right to make that choice between themselves, their doctor, and their faith. Letting other people make decisions of faith on their own, even if their decision disagrees with your own faith, is a reasonable compromise.

It is also time for Pro-choice Americans to realize that late-term abortions that are medically unnecessary are cruel and inhumane. It is not much of a stretch to compromise on that point. The woman can choose to finish out the pregnancy and give the baby up for adoption. It is hard to argue against the sensibility of making a decision to do that instead of having an abortion.

I can tell you right now that the very people who want to force a woman to have the baby will ask, "Who is going to pay for all this healthcare needed? Who is going to pay for all the support a single mother needs to keep her child?" That is the most shameful and cruel aspect about this issue, people want to force a woman to have a child, and once that child is born, those very same people choose to turn their backs on the woman and her newborn. They use their religious beliefs to take a stand against abortion and want to force their religious beliefs onto another person and then ignore their religious tenets to help out their fellow human beings. The mother is left to struggle and care for a child that she wants to keep but can't afford. But we can choose to be better than that. We can choose to compromise. We can choose to love our neighbor. We can choose to do the right thing for each other.

We can set a course where a compromise on abortion is possible and reasonable.

DEMOCRACY

It was probably in the early 90s. I had a customer who had just bought a community newspaper. The kind of newspaper you find thrown in your driveway every week or every other week. He bought the paper I believe so he could be the Editor and write columns on the Editorial page. We talked about politics pretty much on a weekly basis. I remember one time I had mentioned that the Founding Fathers had done such a great job creating the Constitution and how the American form of government was the best in the world. He laughed and replied, telling me that the best form of government is a benevolent dictator. I tilted my head like a puppy dog and had to admit he was right. Then we went on to agree there are no benevolent Dictators in the world and probably never would be, not that we really knew if there had been one or not.

Now that leaves us with what I believe is the second-best form of government when the Constitution is followed and the men and women elected to office are honest people with integrity. The most important characteristic of an elected official has to be their willingness to vote against their own best interests and vote for the best interest of the general public. How about we have benevolent people elected to Congress? Wouldn't a Congress full of elected people doing the right thing for the general public be the best form of government? Most democracies around the world don't work because the people in power are only looking out for their own best interests. When you are only looking out for your own best interest, you are usually, at some point, taking away from someone else's best interest. That is a recipe for failure.

What are the biggest threats to our form of democracy? Misinformation and downright lies are one of them. How about fake news? News that really is fake, or real news that is perceived as fake are both threats to Democracy.

How about elected officials who take an oath to protect the Constitution and then fail to uphold it? How about elected officials who openly violate the Constitution, knowing they have other elected officials who are unwilling to hold them accountable? Are either of those instances a threat to our form of Democracy? I believe they both are.

Is it a threat to Democracy to have a society that tolerates threats and intimidation toward people who are doing the Right and Just work to protect our Constitution? I believe it is. You have to ask yourself, "On whose behalf are they giving out these threats?" The threats and intimidation seem to be more organized these days and not just some random crazy person out there. I believe we need to hold the people accountable on whose behalf these threats are benefiting. How do we hold them accountable? Don't vote for them. Threats and intimidation toward people doing the right thing should not be tolerated. Doing the right thing is always the right thing to do and should not cause you to be a victim of threats and intimidation.

Is it a threat to Democracy to have well-armed militias advocating for violence against government officials and politicians? I believe it is.

Is it a threat to our Democracy to have foreign dictators pulling the strings of our national foreign policy? I believe it is. Are the elected officials who go along with aiding and abetting a foreign government's influence committing acts of treason? I believe they are.

Is it a threat to our Democracy to pass laws making it harder to vote? Is it a threat to our Democracy to consciously and purposely have too few voting machines in areas, causing long lines and waiting times over several hours to vote? It is a threat to our Democracy to have the United States Postal Service's mail sorting machines removed and taken out of service with the purpose to slow down the mail to keep some of the mail-in ballots from being received in time for acceptance? I believe it is.

Is it a threat to our Democracy to have an elected official try and strong-arm a State election official to manufacture thousands of votes to change the results of an election in that State? I believe it is. Is it a threat to our Democracy for elected officials to believe that it is OK to illegally change the vote count in a State to change the results from the rightful winner to someone else? I believe it is. How do we protect our Democracy? Vote them out. Vote out every single one of them and replace them with honest and benevolent elected officials.

Do we want to be the Generation that let our Founding Fathers down and failed to uphold their great experiment known as America? Do we want to be the Generation that let the Constitution fail because we failed to honor it? Do we want to be the Generation that lets down all the young people around the world that want to live in a free and shared society with the mission to better the lives of everyone? We don't have to be that Generation; we can choose not to be that Generation; we can vote to save Democracy; we can vote to save the future of the young people around the world.

We can set a course to where the ideals of Democracy can thrive and succeed.

May God bless all of you and give you the strength to do the Right thing, because doing the Right thing is always the Right thing to do.

SYNOPSIS

Iknow I have put forward a lot of big ideas in a quick and short format. These ideas are meant to move us forward and set a course for America to evolve and succeed. It is time for America to evolve and start a new chapter without tearing down or cutting up its foundational documents. It is time for America to begin a new era free of divisiveness and hatred among its citizens by achieving well-thought-out compromises to its toughest issues. The same issues used to divide us and used to seek power and profits from their exploitation. These issues are big in nature and can only be solved by solutions that are big in nature as well.

There is no role for Religion in Government. There is a role for our collective faith in God in the way we govern ourselves. There is a way to protect our right to adhere to our religious tenets without being overtly discriminatory in the way we conduct business. We must allow businesses to register their discriminatory exceptions at the time of licensing and require them to list these exceptions at the point of entry to their shops, whether they be virtual or physical locations. This way consumers are not blindly seeking products or services at a place of business that will not serve them because the religious beliefs of the consumer do not match up with the religious beliefs of the business owner. Whether you believe in God or you just believe in a common humanity seeking what is Right and Just for every human being, we can all agree that religious beliefs should be held private and be shared with others who share those beliefs.

The answer to protecting the right to bear arms for law-abiding citizens and getting a handle on the availability of guns to be purchased by criminals is to treat guns the same way we treat automobiles with regard to registration and liability. We treat automobiles as deadly weapons and have laws protecting people's rights when injured by an automobile, but we don't treat guns as deadly weapons in the same way. Automobiles and guns cross State lines with little or no regard to how the laws differ from State to State. Let us form a Federal agency called the Department of Motor Vehicles and Firearms, setting the laws and requirements as they pertain to automobiles and firearms at a National level. That way, red and yellow flag restrictions on people can follow a person from State to State and be as effective as possible. Law enforcement officers will have the necessary information when approaching a residence or an automobile as to how many guns are registered to the owner of the house or auto, ultimately saving the lives of first responders who deserve as much information and protection as we can possibly give them. The Founding Fathers were very much in favor of a well-regulated gun ownership policy. They banned the right to bear arms to large classes of people they deemed to be unusually dangerous or unvirtuous. A Florida law in 1825 authorized white people to enter the homes of black people and take away their guns and ammunition. There is a long history of regulations defining who can own guns in this country. And requiring a gun owner to register their guns can be part of a compromise aimed at reducing gun violence in America.

I have had friends ask me, "How do we know what is true and what isn't?" They are frustrated by all the misinformation out there that is being presented as factual and being presented as news. If we can have a rating system for the content of movies and television shows, then we can have a rating system for news shows, talk shows, and podcasts. We can rate them as news shows based on facts, talk shows based on opinion, talk shows based on facts or both, and podcasts based on opinion or facts or both. I believe there is a growing market for these types of broadcasts and these types of broadcasts would be willing to pay a nominal fee to be monitored and rated as a trusted source of news and opinion based on facts.

People have stated for a long time that we need an economy that works for everyone. The accumulation of wealth by the few and the power of big business's ability to control markets has un-leveled the playing field and has all but eliminated small business's ability to compete. That horse is out of the barn and there is no going back. However, we can make some adjustments and put in guardrails and programs to ensure the average worker in America can afford to enjoy the life God has given them. The economic system called Oak Tree Economics, with its programs and guardrails to lower the bar of what is a living wage will do just that, allowing the average American to get ahead financially and be self-sufficient.

Food, shelter, clothing, and healthcare are the four basic needs of any human being to have a standard quality of life that is acceptable. We as a country spend twice as much as other civilized countries per citizen and get much worse results for the money we spend. This is the time when we need to make big sweeping changes to our healthcare system. I have laid out a plan to make those big sweeping changes possible and doable. These changes will lower the cost of healthcare for the individual and for the business owner providing healthcare for their employee. At the same time, providing healthcare to all Americans because all Americans deserve healthcare. We as a country can stay on the path of paying more and getting less for what we spend, or we can make the necessary changes and investments to our healthcare system and get more while paying less.

An education is something every child in America deserves to have. Every child in America is the future of our workforce and public education should be geared to help that child enter the workforce with the ability to succeed and be self-sufficient. The idea that a young person can leave high school after staying for one extra year and be able to work and earn a living wage will lead to less homelessness, less drug addiction, and less suicide across the younger population. Public education needs to be a vehicle by which our economy gains the necessary workforce to be successful and grow.

Climate change is something we can all agree is occurring. What is the cause we can differ on? The overall consensus of most scientists is that the burning of fossil fuels is definitely contributing to the polluting and thinning of our atmosphere. The pollution of our atmosphere is allowing the sun to heat up our one and only planet in ways that are detrimental to the balance of nature. One thing we are sure of, is that the supply of fossil fuels and natural gas is not endless and that the supply of both is running out. We need to be moving away from these resources and moving to resources that are both renewable and good for our planet. The motivation of people to want to use every last drop of oil and every last cubic meter of natural gas must be based on greed and greed alone. Why would we want to ruin the balance of nature as we know it and ruin the quality of life for generations of human beings and animals? We need to vote out the people standing in the way of change and vote for the people who want to save our only planet, so our kids and their kids can have a planet to live on.

I believe it is time to celebrate the differences between Races. It is time for us to accept the different cultures of each Race as unique and personal to the Races themselves. The idea of all of us being equal is a fallacy and it leads to people comparing themselves to others. As people compare themselves to others, it is very natural for people to pass judgment in such a way as to make themselves feel different and superior. If we can move past the idea that we are all equal and move toward the idea we are all human beings deserving of an equal chance at a good life, we can learn to blindly accept our differences and treat others the way we would want to be treated ourselves.

When it comes to Gay marriage, all I can say is when two adults come together to get married in front of the God they believe in, whose place is it for anyone else to say they can't?

The issue of abortion is a tough one to solve. It demands a compromise that leads to far fewer abortions being needed or wanted. It demands a compromise where a young woman knows she can receive the support and assistance she needs to keep the baby. Or it demands a compromise where she has the confidence her baby will be well cared for if she decides to give it up for adoption or foster care. The compromise must allow for an abortion in the first two trimesters due to an unwanted pregnancy or an anytime abortion for medical reasons determined to be necessary by her doctor. Pregnancies are very complicated and nothing less than a miracle when they go smoothly and the mother and infant are both healthy. But when the miracle of birth is not in the stars for the mother, it is important for abortion to be an option. An option decided on by the young woman, her doctor, and the God she believes in.

Finally, we need to remember that Democracy and a Constitution are only as strong as the collective people who choose to uphold it. The words on a piece of paper and the laws those words create are useless if they are not honored and revered. We, as citizens of the United States of America, need to vote for people who will uphold our Constitution and respect the laws of our land. No one is above the law, and we need to vote for people who believe that with all their hearts.

Milton Keynes UK
Ingram Content Group UK Ltd.
UKHW020746071024
449371UK00014B/1062

9 798822 959484